LITTLE
MONSTERS

ALBERT MARRIN

LITTLE MONSTERS

THE CREATURES THAT LIVE ON US AND IN US

DUTTON CHILDREN'S BOOKS
AN IMPRINT OF PENGUIN GROUP (USA) INC.

DUTTON CHILDREN'S BOOKS
A division of Penguin Young Readers Group

Published by the Penguin Group
Penguin Group (USA) Inc., 375 Hudson Street, New York, New York 10014, U.S.A.
Penguin Group (Canada), 90 Eglinton Avenue East, Suite 700, Toronto, Ontario, Canada M4P 2Y3
    (a division of Pearson Penguin Canada Inc.)
Penguin Books Ltd, 80 Strand, London WC2R 0RL, England
Penguin Ireland, 25 St Stephen's Green, Dublin 2, Ireland (a division of Penguin Books Ltd)
Penguin Group (Australia), 250 Camberwell Road, Camberwell, Victoria 3124, Australia
    (a division of Pearson Australia Group Pty Ltd)
Penguin Books India Pvt Ltd, 11 Community Centre, Panchsheel Park, New Delhi - 110 017, India
Penguin Group (NZ), 67 Apollo Drive, Rosedale, Auckland 0632, New Zealand
    (a division of Pearson New Zealand Ltd.)
Penguin Books (South Africa) (Pty) Ltd, 24 Sturdee Avenue, Rosebank, Johannesburg 2196, South Africa

Penguin Books Ltd, Registered Offices: 80 Strand, London WC2R 0RL, England

Every attempt has been made to trace the ownership of all copyrighted material and to secure necessary reprint permissions. In the event of any question arising as to the use of reprinted material, the editor and the publisher, while expressing regret for any inadvertent error, will be happy to make the necessary corrections in future printings. The publisher wishes to thank those institutions who granted permission to reproduce works, and for their kind cooperation in the realization of this book.

Interior photo credits include: Prologue, 8, 23, 35, 50, 54, 67, 74, 94, 98, 110, 136 Photomicrographs copyright 2011 Dennis Kunkel Microscopy, Inc.; page 6, courtesy of Chris Glenn, The University of Queensland; page 10, courtesy of Dr. Matthew Gilligan; pages 21, 24, 25, 62, 63, 132 courtesy of the National Library of Medicine; page 27 courtesy of Professor Robert W. Cohn, ElectroOptics Research Institute and Nanotechnology Center; page 36 courtesy of Steve Gschmeissner / Photo Researchers, Inc.; page 42 courtesy of the Center for Urban & Structural Entomology; page 45 courtesy of Jens Buurgaard Nielsen; page 60, 81, 103, 107, 116, 119, 131 courtesy of the Center for Disease Control; page 71 courtesy of Lennart Nilsson Photography; pages 76, 77 courtesy of the Australian Museum; page 95 courtesy of Ron Dickinson; page 101 courtesy of Science Museum/SSPL; page 121 courtesy of CDC / Photo Researchers, Inc; page 130 courtesy of T.J. Nolan, University of Pennsylvania School of Veterinary Medicine

Library of Congress Cataloging-in-Publication Data

Marrin, Albert.
The creatures that live on us and in us / Albert Marrin. — 1st ed.
p. cm.
Includes bibliographical references and index.
ISBN 978-0-525-42262-4 (hardcover : alk. paper)
1. Parasites—Juvenile literature. I. Title.
QL757.M334 2011
578.6'5—dc22   2009053242

Published in the United States by Dutton Children's Books, a division of Penguin Young Readers Group
345 Hudson Street, New York, New York 10014
www.penguin.com/youngreaders

Printed in China | First Edition
10 9 8 7 6 5 4 3 2 1

come come come
come in your billions
tiny small feet
and humming little wings
crawlers and creepers
wigglers and stingers
scratchers borers slitherers

— **DON MARQUIS**, from
archy and mehitabel, 1927

CONTENTS

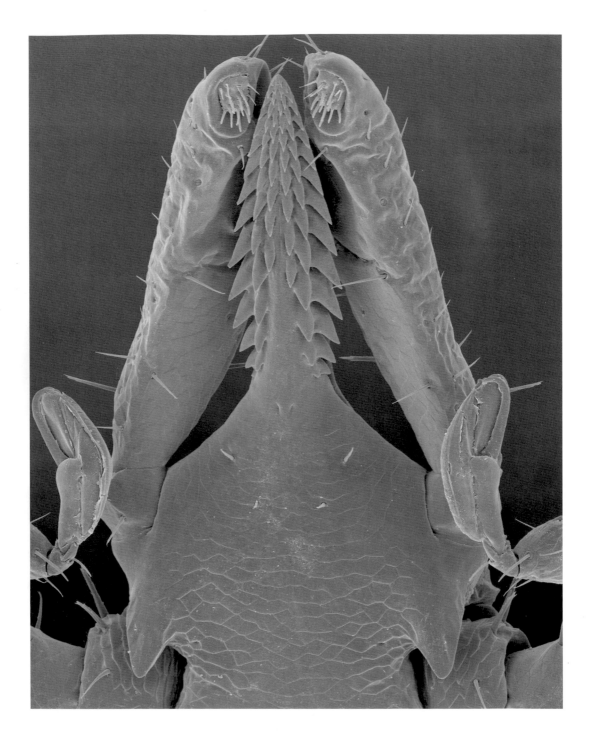

MY FIRST PARASITE

When I was little, my family lived in a crowded New York City neighborhood. Street after street of tall apartment houses stood side by side, stretching into the distance for miles. The streets echoed to the constant rumble of traffic.

Luckily, Van Cortlandt Park lay within walking distance to our street. It was a two-mile walk, but my friends and I went to the park often. It had a swimming pool, running track, tennis courts, and baseball fields. Best of all, it had a vast wild area, where we played "Jungle." We would crawl through the tangled brush or lie still in the tall grass, waiting to shoot each other with toy guns.

Once, as I got ready for bed after a long day of Jungle, I noticed several tiny brownish things clinging to my legs. They had hard shells, and felt like seeds. Yet, when I tried to brush them off, they did not budge. Instead, they seemed to tighten their grip with sharp tongs. It hurt.

"Ticks," said the emergency-room doctor in the local hospital. "Your boy has ticks," he told my father, frowning. As the white-coated man spoke, he held one up with the tweezers he had used to remove it ever so gently. This was my first meeting with a parasite.

The doctor explained that ticks need to attach themselves to warm-blooded creatures like dogs, cats, squirrels—and people. Especially to little boys who play Jungle! Once attached, a tick bites the animal and sucks its blood. When it has taken its fill, the tick, its belly swollen to three times normal size, drops to the ground. After digesting the blood, it will seek another animal for another meal of blood.

Although I went on to become a professor of history, I have been interested in parasites ever since my run-in with those ticks. Over the years, I learned that everyone has parasites of one sort or another. Not only are parasites fascinating in themselves, they have helped shape human history for uncounted generations. This book tells their story.

The head of a deer tick. Note the sawlike mouth. This tick, a blood-sucking arachnid, can spread several diseases to humans and animals.

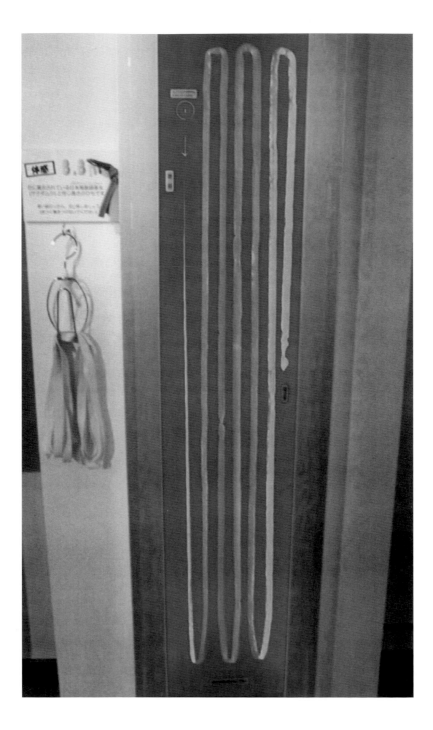

1 Secret Sharers

We are never alone. Wherever we go, whatever we do, other organisms—living beings—are with us always. They are the parasites, our secret sharers.

Every organism has parasites. Animals that live on land have them. Animals that live under the ground have them. Fish have them, and whales, too. Birds have them. Bees have them. Even tiny little fleas have them, and so do humans. Parasites are sneak thieves. They attach themselves to us, bore into our

Adult tapeworm specimen, 346.5 inches long, Meguro Museum of Parasitology, Tokyo.

bodies, take shelter inside us, steal our food, and drink our blood. Sometimes they take our lives.

In science, a *parasite* is an animal or plant that survives by living on or inside another animal or plant. *Parasite* comes from the Greek word *parasitos*, meaning "beside the food." In ancient Greece, wealthy people, to gain respect by being generous, invited poor folk in to have a meal with them. These guests, called *parasitos*, earned their food by praising their hosts, singing, reciting poetry, and telling amusing stories. Gradually, the word's meaning changed. By the 1700s, a parasite was a freeloader, a creature that took from another but gave nothing in return. Today, we call such a person a "social parasite." Japanese people refer to children who live with their parents until their early thirties as "parasitic singles."

Parasites have existed for the longest time. Scientists believe

PARASITOLOGY

All medical schools offer courses in *parasitology*–the branch of biology that studies parasites. Schools of agriculture and veterinary medicine also teach the subject, for crops, farm animals, and pets constantly face attack by parasites. Some nations keep large collections of parasites preserved in alcohol. Specialists use these as references to identify parasites found in people, animals, and plants. The Meguro Museum of Parasitology in Tokyo, Japan, displays only parasites; it has 45,000 specimens. Museum visitors like to have their pictures taken with the 30-foot-long tapeworm, taken from a man's intestines, displayed in the lobby. Yet the Meguro Museum is tiny compared with the U.S. National Parasite Collection. Located in Beltsville, Maryland, it has over 1 million specimens and 25 full-time *parasitologists*, scientists who specialize in the study of parasites. They are busy people.

they go back nearly to the dawn of life on our planet. We may never completely answer the question of how parasites arose. What is certain is that fossils, the hardened remains or traces of ancient creatures, show that even the mighty dinosaurs had parasites.

The fossilized feather of a flying reptile that lived 120 million years ago, for example, has rows of tiny bumps resembling insect eggs. The remains of "Leonardo," a 75-million-year-old duck-billed dinosaur, suggest that this giant had parasites, too. Dug from the rocks of Montana in 2001, Leonardo belongs to a group of plant-eaters that grew to 50 feet in length and weighed over three tons. Fossilized traces of plants found in Leonardo's gut area have hundreds of long, hair-thin white lines, suggesting burrows made by parasitic worms. It is likely that flesh-eating dinosaurs, like the huge *Tyrannosaurus rex* (King tyrant lizard), scratched at skin parasites with their razor-sharp claws and even have been killed by them. More recently, 10,000 years ago, giant elephants called mammoths roamed North America during the Ice Age. Scientists have found insect parasites in the thick wool coats of frozen mammoths.

The ancestors of all parasites were probably free-living organisms that could survive on their own, without needing a host.

While scientists have not found any of their fossilized remains as of yet, it seems likely that various plants and animals became parasitic long before the earliest dinosaurs appeared about 280 million years ago. Parasites probably evolved because the parasitic lifestyle made it easier to survive, by hitching onto other organisms for free meals. Doing so, however, made it necessary to change one's lifestyle, even one's very shape, in basic ways.

Genetics may explain how free-livers became parasites. This branch of biology deals with heredity, or how one generation passes on its traits to the next. It seems likely that genetic mutations from one generation to another allowed parasite ancestors to get a meal more easily. Take worms that fed on the bodies of animals that died on the African plains a million years

Artist's rendition of the head of "Sue," a 42-foot, 7-ton T-Rex that lived in South Dakota 67 million years ago. Scientists believe the holes in the jawbone were the result of infection by a certain single-celled protozoa that is also a bird parasite. It seems that the parasites bored into the giant's jaw and lodged in its throat, causing it to starve to death.

GENES: Blueprints for Parasites (and for You)

Genetics takes its name from the genes, which are bits of a chemical called DNA found in every cell. Cells are the basic units of life; every living being is made up of anywhere from one to several trillion cells. Arranged in long strands, an organism's DNA holds the instructions for how its entire body is built and works. DNA controls body size, shape, color, the senses, movement, digestion, waste removal, reproduction, and many other things. Organisms reproduce by giving copies of their genes to their offspring.

Sometimes offspring do not get exact copies of a gene. Chemical errors in copying or radiation from the sun cause a gene to change, or "mutate."

If the mutation lessens the offspring's ability to survive, it is more likely to die without reproducing, and without passing on the unlucky mutation. A mutation that changes a moth's color ever so slightly, for example, may make it more visible to birds, and thus easier to find and eat. If the mutation gives the organism a survival advantage, on the other hand, it will be more likely to pass on the change to offspring. We see this with moths whose color blends with the bark of the tree they rest on, thus making the moths harder for birds to see. We also see this with bitter-tasting moths that birds instantly spit out of their mouths.

ago. A large predator might also eat the dead animal. Lions, for example, are not only hunters but also scavengers; they ate the carcasses of dead animals along with the worms feeding on the carcass. Eventually, mutations enabled certain worms to adjust to living in a lion's guts. In doing so, they also shed unneeded body parts. For example, nonparasitic worms lack eyes but have sensitive nerves called "receptors," which easily detect light. Since there is no light in a lion's guts, these receptors were

This bird mite lives in the tiny barbs of a bird's feather.

no longer needed. Worms that took up the parasitic lifestyle gradually lost their receptor nerves. In their place, parasitic worms produced chemicals that told them where they were in the host's body.

However it came about, the parasitic lifestyle was a huge success. Parasites are the ultimate survivors, the most common form of life on Earth. There are far more species of parasites than any other organism. Scientists think that over 80 percent of all living things are parasites. Every species of free-living plant or animal may have several different parasites living on or in it at the same time. Take the tiny leopard frog: it can have 12 different parasites, each living in a separate part of its body, and none other. A species of Mexican parrot has 30 different types of parasite on its feathers alone.

Yet that is just the beginning of the story. For parasites often have parasites of their own, and those parasites have parasites, too. Scientists call parasites of parasites "hyperparasites." Think of the cuckoo. This parasitic bird lays a single egg in another bird's nest. The host bird sits on all the eggs, only to have the larger cuckoo chick kill its nest mates after they hatch. Yet the cuckoo has its own parasites: fleas. And those fleas can play host to a dozen species of parasitic worms.

In some ways, survival can be seen as an endless "arms race" between parasite and host. Over millions of years, parasites have gained the ability to control their hosts in various ways. Certain parasites change their hosts' bodies to suit their needs. For instance, some isopods, members of a group of tiny crablike creatures, have given up hunting for food. Instead, one species swims into the mouth of a spotted snapper, a fish many times its size, and snips off the snapper's tongue. The isopod then acts as a tongue, helping the snapper hold its prey, while stealing bits of food for itself. Another species of isopod has discovered how

Isopod takes place of fish tongue.

to "feminize" the male shrimp; that is, change males into females. After doing so, the isopod attaches its young to the shrimp's eggs. Nobody knows how it carries out the sex change.

Parasites have also developed arsenals of chemicals that make hosts change their behavior in strange ways. Such changes are always to the parasites' benefit, never to the hosts'. For example, the young of certain parasitic worms take control of grasshoppers' brains. Upon reaching adulthood, they force their insect hosts to commit suicide by drowning themselves. The worms then swim away to continue their life cycle in the water. Another type of parasitic worm makes host fish swim close to the surface of lakes, where wading birds can easily catch them. The worms then lay their eggs inside the bird. Other parasitic worms prefer ants to fish. Through some type of chemical magic, they force ant hosts to climb to the tip of a blade of grass, exposing themselves to grazing animals. When eaten, the young worms complete their life cycle inside the new host animal.

While some mutations have allowed organisms to become parasites, others have helped hosts fight parasites. Woolly bear caterpillars, for example, have a trick that kills the parasites troubling them. Normally these caterpillars eat plants in the pea family. Yet, if troubled by worms, woolly bears switch to hemlock leaves, which are poisonous to most animals but not to them. The worms die off. Similarly, chimpanzees will change their diet, switching to bitter-tasting plants, to clean out intestinal worms. Sheep infected by intestinal worms may stop eating altogether, or eat very little, until they feel better.

Plants suffer from insect parasites, but may also enlist insect allies against pests. When bitten into by caterpillars, beetles, or bugs, plants cannot cry out in pain. But they can do something just as effective. As an insect feeds on a leaf, the plant may spray tiny droplets of a chemical into the air. The chemical is powerful stuff; indeed, it is a magnet for special types of wasps called "parasitoids," which will kill whatever insect is feeding on the plant.

There are over 200,000 species of wasps, of which at least half are parasitoids. A parasite, we know, lives at a host's expense but usually does not kill it. It makes no sense to destroy the creature you feed on and in which you spend nearly your whole life. Parasitoids, however, always kill their hosts. But not immediately.

Parasitoid wasps speed along the scent trail to the signaling plant. Many species of wasps, bees, and ants have a stinger at the end of their tail. The stinger is a weapon; it injects poison in self-defense or to protect its owner's nests. A female parasitoid, however, has a stinger and an "ovipositor," or egg depositor. While plunging her ovipositor into an insect's body, she inserts several eggs. Before long, the eggs hatch into tiny caterpillars called larvae, which use the host as a living supermarket. Carefully avoiding its vital organs, they slowly eat it alive from the inside. When ready, the larvae chew their way out of their still-living

Wasp cocoons cling to this tomato hornworm.

host to become pupae, the stage in a winged insect's life before adulthood. Left behind when the adult wasp emerges is the dead caterpillar, now merely a dry, sucked-out shell. Laboratories in the United States and Latin America raise parasitoid wasps for sale to farmers to control crop-eating insects. These wasps are more effective and better for the environment than chemical insecticides, which kill economically useful as well as harmful insects.

Some animals use various social behaviors to defend against parasites. Animals that move in herds—elephants, bison, musk oxen—stand next to each other, swishing their tails or stamping their feet to ward off troublesome insects. Other animals groom each other. When not eating or sleeping, all species of monkeys spend their time picking skin parasites off each other. Grooming gets rid of parasites, and also strengthens the bonds between group members.

TYPES OF PARASITES
Parasites relate to their hosts in various ways.

ECTOPARASITES are outsiders; that is, they live on or in their host's skin. Fleas and lice are well-known examples of ectoparasites.

ENDOPARASITES, on the other hand, are insiders, living within the bodies of their hosts. Tapeworms are the largest endoparasites.

Finally, **TEMPORARY PARASITES** live apart from their hosts most of the time, visiting them only to feed. Ticks, leeches, and bedbugs are examples of temporary parasites.

Like any animal, humans share their bodies with other

living beings. A few of these are fungi, members of the same "kingdom," or large grouping, as mushrooms. Fungi feed on plant and animal matter, both living and dead. In humans, they cause annoying infections such as athlete's foot, jock itch, and ringworm. Ringworm looks like a parasitic worm curled just under the skin's surface, but is really a fungus.

Most human parasites belong to two kingdoms. Protozoa are single-celled organisms. Some of these tiny creatures, of which there are over 80,000 species, have brought humanity more misery and death than anything else in our history, including

CARL LINNAEUS
devised the system of scientific classification of living beings.

How many living species exist today?

KINGDOM	ESTIMATED NUMBER OF SPECIES
Bacteria	4,000
Protozoa	80,000
Animals (with backbones)	52,000
Animals (without backbones)	1,272,000
Fungi	72,000
Plant	270,000
Total number of described species	1,750,000
Possible number of unknown species.	14,000,000

(Source: "Insect Taxonomy and Classification," einsteins-emporium.com/life/animal-info/insects/taxonomy.htm)

NAMING NAMES

In the eighteenth century, the Swedish naturalist Carl Linnaeus (1707–78) invented a method of giving organisms scientific names. His method allows people in any part of the world, speaking any language, to understand each other when referring to an organism.

Since Linnaeus's day, scientists have arranged, or classified, all organisms into various groupings that have certain basic things in common, such as whether or not they have a backbone. Scientists call the largest groupings **kingdoms.** All living beings belong to one of five kingdoms:

- **Monera** (bacteria, the simplest single-celled life-forms)
- **Protist** (protozoa, microscopic single-celled creatures such as amoebas)
- **Fungi** (fungi, mosses, molds, yeasts, mushrooms)
- **Plantae** (plants)
- **Animalia** (animals)

Each kingdom has smaller groups, which share even more things in common:

    Phylum (plural, phyla)
      Class
        Order
          Family
            Genus (plural, genera)
              Species

So, for example, species of the same genus are more closely related and more alike than species of the same family, and so on. Only members of the same species can mate and reproduce their own kind.

Just as most people have a first and last name, each species is also "binomial" or two-named. These names are usually given in Latin or Greek, once the common languages of learned people. Each name is written in italics. The first word, the genus name, starts with a capital letter. The second word, or species name, is written in lowercase letters.

For example, scientists classify our own species, *Homo sapiens,* this way:

- **Kingdom:** Animalia
- **Phylum:** Chordata (animals with a spinal cord that extends from the brain down through the backbone, its branches forming the nervous system)
- **Class:** Mammalia (animals whose mothers feed their young milk from their mammae, or breasts)
- **Order:** Primates (mammals with grasping hands and fingers, like monkeys)
- **Family:** Hominidae (mammals with upright posture and large brains, humans and their nearest prehuman ancestors)
- **Genus:** Homo, meaning "man"
- **Species:** sapiens, meaning "wise"

wars and famines. As we will see, a protozoan causes malaria, the worst killer of all time. Other human parasites belong to branches of the animal kingdom, including insects and their relatives, such as mites, ticks, and worms. Scientists believe that for many parasites, humans are the ideal host.

Nature composes some of her loveliest music
for the microscope and the telescope.

— THEODORE ROSZAK, professor of history,

Where the Wasteland Ends (1972)

2 Learning About Parasites

Although people have always suffered from parasites, it is only in the last three centuries that we have been able to study them and learn how they live. How we learned about parasites is one of the great adventure stories of all time.

The earliest true humans, *Homo sapiens*, appeared in East Africa about 150,000 years ago. From there, small bands of hunter-explorers slowly spread worldwide. Scientists studying our earliest history have found human bones in caves and

Hippocrates, the ancient Greek physician credited with founding the study of disease in humans.

prehistoric campsites, along with dried human feces. Under close examination in the laboratory, ancient feces show that our ancestors had parasitic worms.

More recently, some 7,500 years ago, peoples in Egypt and South America believed the spirits of the dead might live forever in the next world. For that to happen, however, their bodies needed to be preserved as mummies. A mummy is an embalmed body, or a body preserved naturally in a dry climate. Upon examination, scientists have found microscopic worm eggs in hundreds of mummies.

The first written accounts of diseases possibly caused by parasites come from Egyptian records of around 3000–2500 B.C. Later, ancient Greek physicians, notably Hippocrates, "the father of medicine," also described infections very likely caused by parasites. So did old-time Chinese and Arab physicians.

Early physicians had no idea of where parasites came from or how they lived. In part, the reason lay in general ignorance about the origin of life. Even learned people thought life arose through "spontaneous generation." This is the belief that living organisms arise from nonliving things. Thus, according to ancient science, frogs supposedly grew from muddy soil, flies came from rotting meat, and garbage turned into rats. Nor could anyone imagine how many types of parasites there were. True, you cannot miss a foot-long Guinea worm as it slithers out of the hole it made in your leg. Yet most parasites are invisible to the naked eye, especially in the early stages of their life cycles. To see them, you need a microscope. As it would be thousands of years before the invention of the microscope, these early doctors had no idea that tiny parasites were the causes of many diseases.

Diagram dating from the late 1600s of an early model of an optical microscope.

Robert Hooke, English pioneer in the scientific life of the microscope.

The lenses of microscopes are made out of glass. People had known how to make glass since ancient times. The Greeks and Romans made glass drinking vessels—"glasses"—and used colored glass for decorations. By the late 1200s, craftspeople were making spectacles—"eyeglasses"—by grinding pieces of clear glass into lenses, so called because they were shaped like lentil seeds. Lenses were used as magnifying glasses or to start fires by focusing the sun's rays on a piece of wood or paper, thus the name "burning glasses." However, about the year 1590, Dutch spectacle maker Zacharias Janssen and his father, Hans, mounted a lens at either end of a short metal tube. Were they surprised at the result! Anything they placed directly in front of the tube became enlarged up to nine times. They had made the first microscope. At about the same time, inventors placed lenses at the end of long metal tubes and looked at the sky. They had made the first telescopes.

Robert Hooke (1635–1703), an English chemist and inventor, improved on the Janssens' basic design. The hairs on Hooke's head nearly stood up the first time he peered into his microscope. Later, he reported how "by the help of Microscopes there is nothing so small as to escape our inquiry." Aided by his microscopes, Hooke made detailed drawings of fleas and lice, and even the eyes of flies. Placing thin slices of cork taken from the inner bark of an oak tree in front of a microscope, the inventor saw countless tiny hollow boxes. He coined the word *cells* to describe the boxes, because they reminded him of monks' cells in a monastery.

Anton van Leeuwenhoek was the first to use microscopes to see organisms invisible to the naked eye.

Yet the real breakthrough in microscope design came from across the English Channel, in Holland. Anton van Leeuwenhoek (Layu-wen-hook) was a draper, or cloth merchant, in the city of Delft. Like all cloth merchants, Leeuwenhoek (1632–1723) priced his fabrics according to the number of stitches per square inch. The more stitches, the finer the fabric, and the higher the price. To make the counting easier, he used a microscope he had bought somewhere.

The microscope changed everything for Leeuwenhoek. It took over his life. He spent every spare moment peering into its tube. "My work," he recalled after becoming famous, "was not pursued in order to gain the praise I now enjoy, but chiefly from a craving after knowledge. . . . Whenever I found out anything remarkable, I have thought it my duty to put down my discovery on paper, so that all ingenious people might be informed thereof."

Dissatisfied with the microscope he had purchased, Leeuwenhoek found that he had a natural gift for grinding lenses. Before long, he was making his own microscopes. These enlarged objects 275 times, a fantastic accomplishment, while giving the clearest images ever. The Dutchman kept his grinding methods secret; they are still a mystery. What is not a mystery is the way he used microscopes. Hooke and others had studied tiny details of things already visible to the naked eye. Leeuwenhoek went further. His studies revealed another world entirely, one of invisible life-forms he called "animalcules"— very tiny animals.

In the eighteenth century, Dutchman Anton van Leeuwenhoek became the first human to see bacteria and red blood cells. Among his microscopic discoveries was Giardia lamblia, a parasite that lives in water.

Leeuwenhoek placed whatever would fit under his microscopes. While studying a drop of filthy canal water for the first time, he sat back in stunned amazement. That single drop held millions of "very little living animalcules, very prettily a-moving." The largest ones "had a very strong and swift motion, and shot through the water like a pike does through the water."

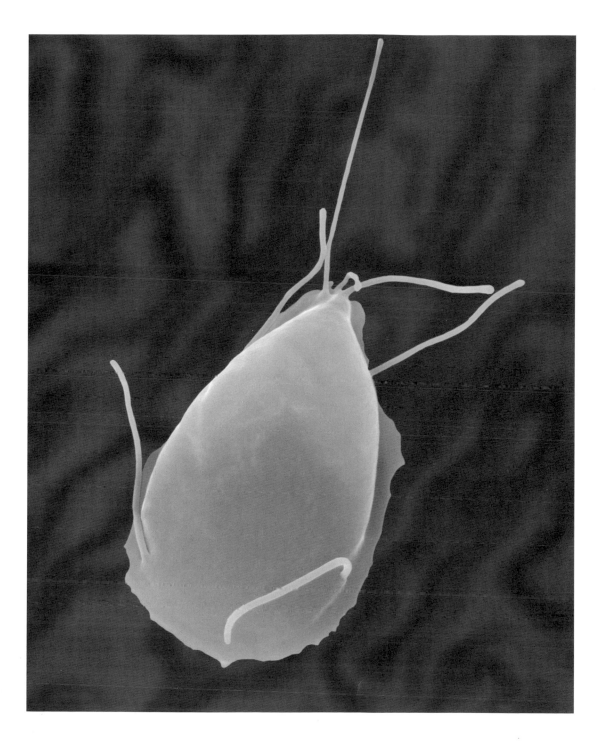

Francesco Redi challenged but did not definitively disprove the theory of spontaneous generation.

Other animalcules "spun around like a top." Over the years, the Dutchman became the first human to see bacteria and red blood cells. While examining his own feces, he discovered *Giardia lamblia*, a common protozoan parasite that lives in water and causes diarrhea in humans.

Leeuwenhoek was more than an inventor and observer. He was a scientific rebel who rejected the idea of spontaneous generation. His microscope studies showed that insects grew from eggs, not dirt, as commonly believed. Francesco Redi (1626–97), an Italian doctor, supported the Dutchman's conclusion. In 1668, Redi showed that meat protected from flies by a layer of finely woven gauze did not become infested with maggots, the immature, wormlike stage of flies, while unprotected meat did. Yet neither man ended the debate over spontaneous generation.

Louis Pasteur (1822–95) had the last word on this subject. In 1864, the French chemist and medical researcher who had already found a cure for rabies made a famous experiment. Pasteur filled a glass flask with meat broth, heating it to kill any bacteria inside.

Then he heated the neck of the flask, carefully bending it into an S-shaped curve. So, while air could reach the broth, airborne bacteria got caught in the curve. As Pasteur expected, nothing grew in the sterile broth. But when he tipped the flask so that the broth flowed into the curved area, it became cloudy with bacteria.

Pasteur's experiment convinced most scientists that new life comes from existing life, not dead matter. It

Louis Pasteur at work in laboratory in the Institut Pasteur, Paris.

also followed that living organisms, not magic or evil spirits, cause disease. This finding scared the daylights out of the great scientist. Pasteur began to act strangely, avoiding shaking hands, even inspecting every slice of bread put on the table, out of fear of dirt and infection. Yet his discoveries marked a turning point in the age-old struggle against disease. Because these proved that diseases have natural causes, humans began to realize that they could study, treat, prevent, and perhaps eliminate them. These ideas lay behind all modern medical research.

Microscopes steadily improved in the centuries following Leeuwenhoek's death. Yet even the best glass-lens devices can enlarge objects only a few hundred times. In the 1930s, a new invention, the scanning electron microscope (SEM), magnified objects millions of times.

Better microscopes and Pasteur's findings encouraged more scientists to make parasites their life's work. By the late 1800s, they were poring over countless glass slides, collecting parasites in all parts of the world, and experimenting with them. These researchers had much in common: curiosity, patience, courage.

Some parasite experiments demanded real bravery, if not recklessness. Take Shimesu Koino, a Japanese baby doctor turned parasitologist. In 1922, Koino mapped the life cycle of a parasitic worm by swallowing its larvae, then recording their effects on him in a daily record. He survived by eventually taking a painful drug to rid his body of the parasites. Earlier, in the 1880s, a professor in

THE ELECTRON MICROSCOPE

Electrons are negative charges of electricity that travel around the center, or nucleus, of atoms. Atoms are the basic building blocks of matter. In 1931, German engineers Ernst Ruska and Max Knoll built the first electron microscope. By focusing a beam of electrons on an object, they were able to project an image of its smallest details, magnified a million times, onto a screen. Since then, electron microscopes have improved to the point where they can magnify objects up to 2 million times. Researchers use electron microscopes to examine biological specimens, find cancer cells in samples of human body tissue, and learn how to make metals purer and stronger. The only problem is that electron beams are so intense that they kill living specimens, making it impossible to see their ever-changing movements.

A researcher sitting before the monitor of a scanning electron microscope.

Germany did something that would never meet today's ethical standards. Without telling him what he was doing, Friedrich Küchenmeister fed pig meat containing immature tapeworms to a criminal condemned to death. Weeks later, after the execution, he recovered adult tapeworms from the man's intestines.

Modern parasitologists recognize that they have only scratched the surface. Surely, hundreds if not thousands of human parasites will be found in the coming years. Equally important, treatments for parasite infections that are effective today may not work tomorrow. Mutations guarantee that some parasites will develop resistance to antibiotics and other drugs. So the arms race continues.

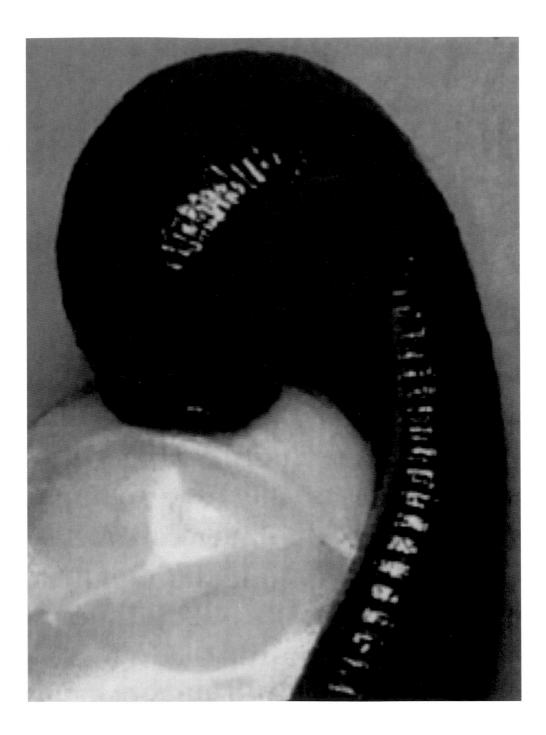

3 Worlds Within Worlds

Each of us is like a miniature planet Earth. Like our home world, our bodies have rivers, jungles, mountains, valleys, and caverns. Like Earth, too, our "geography" is home to a vast array of life forms. Among these are the creatures that live on us for their entire lives or for just brief periods. Others do not live on us at all, but very close to us, visiting when we least expect them. Some of them may be beneficial, but none are pleasant.

This leech has attached itself to the tip of a man's finger.

LEECHES

The April 1854 issue of *Scientific American* magazine printed a report by a doctor recently returned from India. "Leeches," he wrote, "swarmed in incredible profusion in the streams and damp grass, and among the bushes; they got into my hair, hung on my eyelids, and crawled up my legs and down my back. I repeatedly took upwards of a hundred from my legs."

Few ectoparasites give one the "creeps" as leeches do. Leeches live in moist vegetation or marshes, but also in shallow streams, lakes, and along seashores. Like earthworms, their nearest relatives, their bodies have a series of ringlike sections called segments. Unlike earthworms, which eat decaying plant matter, all 650 species of leeches prey on other creatures. Most leeches eat other worms, snails, and insects. A few are parasites, feeding only on the blood of reptiles, fish, birds, and mammals.

Cold and slimy to the touch, leeches have a sucker formed by circular muscles at each end of their body. The rear sucker is used for balance while moving. The front sucker, with the mouth at its center, is for feeding. Nearly all creatures with jaws have two jaws that form the framework of the mouth. Leeches, however, have three jaws holding razor-sharp teeth arranged to make a Y-shaped bite.

Even strong animals are helpless against soft-bodied leeches.

To survive, they have developed various chemicals to solve special problems. First, a host feeling painful bites might become frantic and try to brush off the leeches violently, crushing them. To prevent this, glands in the leech's mouth release a numbing chemical into its saliva so the victim cannot feel the bite. Second, the leech must get as much blood as possible, as quickly as possible. To do that, its saliva has a chemical that dilates, or widens, the blood vessels near the wound, allowing more blood to flow. A third chemical, called hirudin, prevents the blood from thickening or clotting. When the leech has taken its fill, it drops off, but because of hirudin the wound continues oozing blood for up to 24 hours. Finally, bacteria in the leech's gut aid digestion and produce an antibiotic that kills harmful bacteria. Leeches may take five times their body's weight in blood, after which they can go a year without feeding.

ODD LEECH FACTS

A thousand years ago, barbers in Europe were called barber-surgeons. Not only did they use razors to draw blood, they applied leeches to ailing customers. The red stripes on barber poles symbolize this bloodletting. While a leech needs to feed only once a year, doctors nowadays have found a way to reuse them quickly after they have helped a patient. Laboratory workers put blood-swollen leeches into a chemical bath that causes them to vomit. After a day's rest, the leeches can be reused.

Leeches have always had a bad reputation. Some say— wrongly—that they suck their victims dry. Yet, although they might be a nuisance in certain areas of the world, leeches cause no diseases; nor are they vectors for other parasites. (*For more on vectors, see sidebar, page 57.*) If you should find a leech on your skin, keep calm. Do not try to burn it off or pull it off, as burning and pulling leaves the teeth in the wound, causing infection. Applying a few drops of alcohol will make the leech drop off at once.

Despite their evil reputation, these parasites deserve our respect. *Leech* comes from the Old English word for physician. Doctors have used them to treat the sick throughout history. For over two thousand years, bleeding was a favorite treatment for most illnesses; it was supposed to release "evil spirits" from a patient's body. During George Washington's last illness, doctors opened the great man's veins with scalpels four times, draining half his blood. If this did not kill Washington, it did not make him stronger, either. Similarly, applying bloodsucking leeches to various parts of the body supposedly "cured" headaches, eye diseases, mental illness, stomach cramps, and obesity. It did nothing of the sort.

One species deserves its Latin name, *Hirudo medicinalis*, the "medical leech." In the 1980s, doctors turned to this brown creature, less than an inch long, for help with an important problem. Microsurgeons are experts at reattaching fingers, hands, ears, toes, and other body parts lost in accidents. While operating, a surgeon may have trouble connecting the two ends of cut veins, thin-walled vessels that return blood to the heart. The blood going to a reattached ear, say, may clot in a narrow vein, causing the ear to die for lack of oxygen. Enter *Hirudo medicinalis*. The hirudin in this leech's saliva dissolves the clot, allowing oxygen-rich blood to enter the area until the veins heal naturally. In the future, hirudin may also help in heart transplant surgery, an operation that saves thousands of lives every year. Of course, a surgeon cannot put leeches directly into a patient's heart. But laboratory workers can "milk" leeches for their hirudin, which can then be injected into a blood vessel to prevent the formation of clots.

ARTHROPODS

The word *arthropod* (AHR-thruh-pod) is Greek for "jointed foot." However, it is the arthropods' legs, not their feet, that have joints. Instead of bone skeletons to support their bodies from inside, as mammals have, these animals have a hard outer covering or external skeleton. Lobsters and spiders are familiar examples. In this chapter, we are interested in three types of parasitic arthropods—mites, ticks, and insects. While insects have six legs, their arthropod cousins, including spiders, have eight.

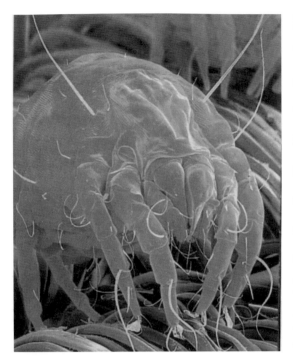

Face to face with a dust mite. Up close and personal, thanks to the electron microscope.

MITES

The Old English word mite means anything small, like a coin of little value. Scientists date the earliest mite fossils to about 400 million years ago, long before the first dinosaurs appeared. Today, some 30,000 species of these eight-legged creatures live just about anywhere you can imagine. Mites have been found in freshwater streams, ponds, lakes, and even hot springs with water over 100 degrees. Most mites feed on plants, some doing serious damage to crops. Others are animal parasites. Lizards have parasitic mites. Honeybees have them, too. So do we.

Dust Mites

One mite species does not live on us, but beside us. You must look at the dust in your house to see why that is a good thing. If not removed every week, the dust accumulates, getting deep enough to write your name in it. You may also notice that, while the living-room carpet is perhaps red and the sofa yellow, the dust is always gray. Why?

Because it's mostly you! Household dust is over 85 percent human skin. (The rest is generally food crumbs, hair, cockroach feces, and cloth fibers.) The body of an adult person is covered by about six square feet of skin. Our skin is our first line of defense, a shield against harmful bacterial invaders. Human skin consists of trillions of cells. These cells are constantly wearing out and dying. Every hour of our lives, no fewer than 1.5 million dead cells peel off our bodies, replaced by new cells that grow beneath the skin's surface. Whenever you move, you shed dead skin cells. In daylight, you see them floating like tiny snowflakes in sunbeams. At night, they glisten in the rays of electric lights. The dust that rises when you beat a mattress or pillow is almost entirely you. Dandruff is merely a clump of dead skin cells on your scalp.

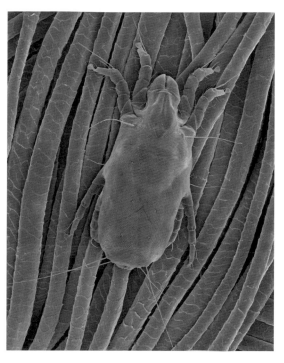

A dust mite seen from above.

Visible only under a microscope, the dust mite is an ugly beast. Yet we cannot do without it. Luckily, it is an eating machine that keeps us from drowning in our own cast-off skin cells. Its favorite hangouts are where we spend most of our time at home. These mites reproduce in fantastic numbers. A square

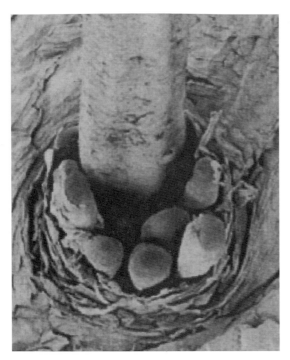

Follicle mites cluster around a hair in its follicle.

yard of carpet may easily harbor 10,000 of them. The mattress you sleep on has anywhere from 100,000 to 10 million of them. While dust mites do not bite or burrow into your body, they have the nasty habit of relieving themselves about 20 times a day. Day in and day out, their droppings accumulate. If your pillow is two years old, for example, 10 percent of its weight is mite feces and dead mites. While dust mites have not been found to carry disease, scientists believe their droppings may cause allergic reactions like sneezing, watery eyes, and skin rashes.

Follicle Mites

A cousin of the dust mite called the follicle mite lives directly on the human body. It makes its home at the base of our facial hairs, especially our eyelashes and eyebrows. Each hair grows from a narrow "cave," or follicle, into which an oil gland empties. Follicle mites are tiny; an adult is less than half the size of the period at the end of this sentence. As many as four mites live head down in a single follicle, gripping the hair with the claws on their legs.

When mature, they leave their home to mate, then find another follicle for the females to lay their eggs in.

Nobody knows what follicle mites eat. Whatever it is, they seem to do nothing else but eat and reproduce. Since they have no anus, they cannot eliminate solid wastes. Perhaps they die of constipation. Anyhow, we do not feel them, since they move too slowly to disturb the nerves in our skin. The best way to keep their numbers down is to wash your face with soap and water, thoroughly and often. Yet washing will not get rid of them entirely, however much we try. Besides causing some people's eyelashes to fall out, these tiny creatures seem harmless. Nearly all humans have follicle mites without knowing it.

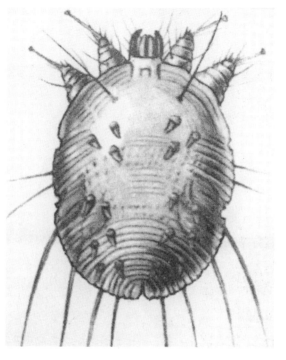

A scabies mite.

Scabies Mites

The same cannot be said about scabies; if you have them, you can't miss them. Scabies (SKAY-beez) mites are barely one-fiftieth of an inch long. They live on and in the skin of humans and animals, including dogs, cats, pigs, and apes. Small as they are, these mites can burrow into any part of your body from your neck to your toes. Usually, however, they favor the skin between your fingers, under your arms, and on your wrists, elbows, waist, shoulders, and back. Wherever they are, scabies cause terrible itching. A baby in its cradle may have scabies mites over its entire body.

As a female scabies mite digs her skin burrow, she lays thousands of microscopic eggs. When the eggs hatch five days later, the young leave the burrow to mate, then dig burrows of their own. Scabies mites multiply quickly. In the most serious cases, a person's skin thickens to form a hard crust riddled with burrows housing upwards of three million mites. Highly contagious, the mites spread through close contact. Simply shaking hands or hugging will not spread them. Sleeping in the same bed as an infected person, or sharing their clothing, will. Doctors use various lotions to kill the mites and relieve the itching they cause. Nasty as they are, they do not seem to carry any diseases that we know of.

Ticks

Ticks are merely large (easily visible to the naked eye) mites that cling to tall grass, bushes, and low tree branches. When an animal brushes against a waiting tick's perch, the tick grabs hold with its sharp claws, which resemble barbed fishhooks. Different tick species prefer different animal hosts: birds, deer, cattle, horses, dogs, chipmunks, squirrels, and mice. Yet ticks are not fussy; they will latch onto any human who comes along. Unlike most mite species, which feed on plant juices, ticks feed only on blood.

Ticks stab into their hosts' flesh with their snout, a miniature double-edged "saw" blade tipped by a needlelike point. That snout can do terrible things. Tribes in Turkestan, a region in Russian Central Asia, used to torture prisoners to death with ticks. Jailers would chain a prisoner to a board in a cell, then release swarms of ticks specially raised and kept hungry for the purpose. Slowly, painfully, they drained the prisoner's blood.

The doubled-edged "saw" snout of a tick.

Patient creatures, ticks can go seven years without a blood meal. After a meal, they let go and drop to the ground to mate.

Unlike their smaller cousins the mites, ticks carry bacteria that cause diseases in animals. Should an infected tick bite a person, he or she will get the disease, too. In the United States, the most common tick-borne diseases are Rocky Mountain spotted fever and Lyme disease.

Dog ticks carry the bacteria that cause Rocky Mountain spotted fever. Pioneers moving westward first met and named the disease in the 1840s while crossing the Rockies. Its symptoms include rashes (spots) on the arms and legs, high fever, and splitting headaches. Nowadays, thanks to antibiotic drugs, few people die of the infection.

Lyme disease gets its name from the Connecticut town that reported the first cases, among children, in 1975. Since then, the infection has spread across the Northeastern, Midwestern, and Pacific Coast states. Deer ticks carry the disease-causing bacteria. Normally the size of pinheads, the black tick doubles in size after a blood meal. Lyme disease symptoms include a circular "bull's-eye" rash, high fever, pounding headaches, and muscle aches. Unless treated early with antibiotic drugs, the infection can seriously damage the heart and brain, and even cause death.

INSECTS

Life as we know it could not exist without insects. Insects help us in countless ways. Bees pollinate our crops and give us honey. Silkworms, really moth larvae, give us a strong fiber that can be woven into beautiful fabric. Ants turn the soil, bringing to the surface minerals plants need to grow. Best of all, insects serve as food for the fish, birds, and animals humans depend upon. Yet it is no accident that we also use the slang expression "you bug me" for those people who annoy, irritate, or pester us. Insects "bug" us. They eat our crops and invade our homes. They can also live on us and bring us untold suffering.

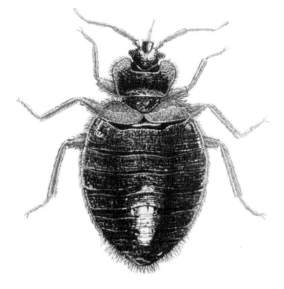

A nasty critter, the sneaky bedbug, feeds on human blood.

Bedbugs

Take the bedbug. I have never heard a good word about this insect. The wingless bedbug has a small head and a needle-sharp beak. Its rust-brown body is the size of an apple seed and shaped like a flattened football—the better to hide in tight spaces. Like the tick, it feeds only on blood.

Originally, bedbugs seem to have tormented large animals,

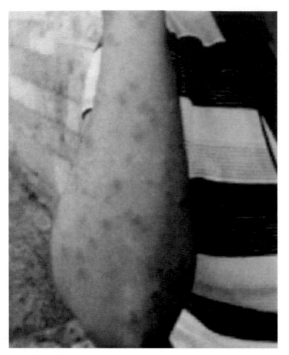

Lines of bedbug bites on a man's arm.

particularly bears, not humans. For thousands of years, our ancestors were nomads, wanderers who hunted animals and gathered wild plants for food. Bedbugs never venture far from their birthplace on their own, so they probably did not bother these early nomadic humans. However, once people began living in caves, the resident bedbugs found them easy, tasty prey. Later, when people took up farming and built permanent houses, the bedbugs came along with them. Now they depend on us entirely, living only in our homes.

Dirt does not attract these pests; they thrive just as easily in the cleanest as in the dirtiest homes. Bedbugs hate light. In daytime, they hide in mattress seams, box springs, bed frames, wall cracks, carpeting, even inside telephones and alarm clocks. At night, the scent of sleepers calls them from their lairs.

It has always been hard to follow this age-old advice: "Sleep tight and don't let the bedbugs bite." Most people cannot sleep soundly, knowing bedbugs are around. And they *will* bite. Should they wake you and you turn on a light, they scoot away; bedbugs are very fast. After you fall asleep again, they return. Bedbugs usually bite three times in a straight line. Some people jokingly call the bites "breakfast, lunch, and supper." Besides the red, itchy bite marks, you know bedbugs are near by their sweet musty odor. Another sure sign of their presence is the sticky black spots—bedbug feces rich in digested blood—found on bedsheets.

Thanks to the insecticide DDT, between the 1950s and the late 1990s bedbugs all but disappeared in the United States and Europe. Recently, however, they have made a strong comeback. This is probably due to mutations that help them resist DDT. Luckily, bedbugs, like mites, transmit no known disease, a fact that does not let us sleep any more soundly.

Even though they are not seriously harmful, the thought of sharing your body with creatures like bedbugs can be terrifying. Everybody occasionally gets itching, prickling, and creeping feelings on their skin. These feelings are normal, arising from common household chemicals like ammonia and hair spray, static electricity, even tiny paper fragments. Fear of parasites, however, gives some people the delusion (false belief) that bedbugs and other parasites infest their skin. That, in turn, may lead to odd behavior. For example, a doctor reported that a patient "spends her entire time from early morning to late at night cleaning, scrubbing, and sterilizing her home." Another patient "boiled the entire family wardrobe each night and all the bedclothes each morning. She insisted that the family bathe in gasoline daily and rub with sulfur and lard "to remove 'invisible' skin parasites."

Flies

Another insect, the fly, has been around for at least 225 million years. Unlike other winged insects with *fly* in their names—butterfly, dragonfly, firefly, mayfly—the "true fly" has just one pair of wings, while the others have two pairs. Flies' nearest relatives are mosquitoes, gnats, and midges. They live everywhere except Antarctica, the ice-covered continent that includes the South Pole.

There are about 125,000 species of flies. Most do not bother humans at all; they live out their lives without our ever noticing them. Others help us by pollinating plants. A few species, like fruit flies, spoil our crops. The common housefly carries bacteria on the hairs of its legs. When a housefly lands on your food, it leaves some of these bacteria behind. This, in turn, may cause food poisoning.

Our ancestors hated flies. The earliest written records, from ancient Egypt, reveal that priests shaved their entire bodies so that flies should not make them "impure" while praying to the gods. Egyptians probably invented the flyswatter; the

Some blowflies have shiny metallic green or blue bodies.

earliest ones have been found in tombs dating from 2500 B.C. The Israelites spoke of the devil as the Lord of the Flies.

People in many countries regard flies as symbols of death. In America, an old children's poem tells what happens when you die:

They wrap you in a big white sheet,
And bury you down six feet deep.
The worms crawl in, the worms crawl out,
They turn your guts to sauerkraut.
They eat your eyes, they eat your nose,
They eat the jelly between your toes.

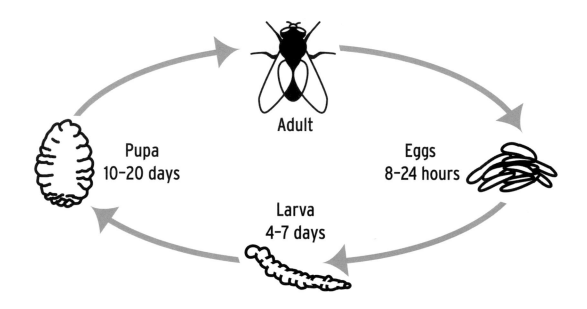

Blowfly life cycle

Maggots

The "worms" mentioned in this poem are maggots, the larvae or immature stage every species of fly must go through. Maggots are usually white, have soft bodies, and no legs. They move by wriggling their bodies back and forth. The females of some species lay their eggs on dead animals, providing a ready source of food for their young when they hatch. Chemicals in the maggots' saliva turn rotting flesh into a paste or liquid, which they slurp up with spongelike mouthparts.

The maggots of certain fly species live as temporary parasites on living animals, including humans. Their parents are bluebottles and green blowflies, winged jewels with gleaming blue and green bellies. An infected wound oozing pus attracts the female flies like honey attracts grizzly bears. The odor given off by decay-causing bacteria draws them from long distances. Quickly, a female lays a batch of eggs in the wound. The warmth of the host's body hatches the eggs, and the maggots feast on any decaying flesh they find.

The thought of maggots eating human flesh makes most people cringe in horror, but these creatures have a good side, too. The police use maggots in a special way. As a dead body decays, different insects, mostly flies, lay eggs on it at different times. For example, houseflies visit fresh corpses and none other. With further decay, bluebottles and others arrive on

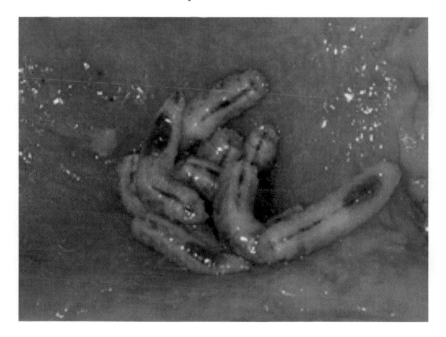

Maggots cleaning a wound by eating infected tissue.

The dark area of this map shows the range of the tsetse fly in Africa.

the scene. Police laboratories can fix the time of death based on the species of fly larvae found on the body at the time of its discovery.

For centuries, wounded soldiers have owed their lives to flies. Wounded men found days after a battle usually had badly infected wounds. Although their wounds swarmed with maggots, these soldiers recovered faster and in larger numbers than those brought quickly to army hospitals. Why?

During World War I, Dr. William S. Baer, a U.S. Army surgeon, found the answer. In 1918, Baer saw a soldier with "thousands and thousands of maggots" in a gaping leg wound. There was such a seething white mass that he could not see any flesh. After removing the young insects one by one with forceps, Baer was startled to find the entire wound area "covered with the most beautiful pink healthy tissue one could imagine." The reason, Baer discovered in a series of experiments, was that maggots are fussy eaters. They love the taste of decay, and nothing else. So they eat only decayed flesh, ignoring healthy flesh. Better yet, maggot saliva is rich in allantoin, a chemical that kills bacteria, which prevents the spread of infection as they chomp away.

No surgeon has eyes keen enough to identify every bit of decay in a wound. As a result, surgeons may need to cut away extra "margin"—healthy-looking tissue—just to be sure. Maggots, however, eat only unhealthy tissue. They are such fussy eaters that they will eat an infected cell, but leave the healthy cell next to it alone.

In treating wounds like bone infections, surgeons may apply maggots rather than scalpels. The number of maggots used depends on how serious the infection is. An infected fingertip may need only five maggots, but an infected stab wound 500 maggots. The white creatures feed for three days, growing fat on decayed flesh, before being removed. Most patients say they do not mind the "tickling" sensation of maggots wriggling in a wound. In 2004, the U.S. Food and Drug Administration gave permission for laboratories to raise and sell "medical maggots." Hundreds of hospitals now treat infections with these temporary parasites.

Sleeping Sickness

Flies have parasites, too. One fly parasite causes a disease described by the Arab historian Ibn Khaldun. "Those afflicted," he wrote in 1390, "are virtually never awake or alert. The sickness harms the patient and continues until he perishes." Now called sleeping sickness, the disease is present in East and Central African countries, including Uganda, Kenya, and Ethiopia. The World Health Organization reports that about 70,000 people die of sleeping sickness every year. In its animal form, the disease kills nearly 3 million cattle a year. In poor countries, the loss of so much livestock is a serious blow to the food supply.

Two species of protozoa of the genus *Trypanosoma* (try-PAN-o-SO-ma) are the villains in sleeping sickness. The name of this group of single-celled animals is Greek for a body shaped like a hole-boring tool. Trypanosomes are living drills. Long and

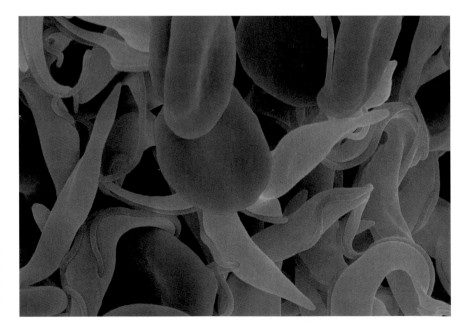

Trypanosoma, a type of protozoa, are infected by the tsetse fly, causing sleeping sickness.

pointed in shape, they move by means of a whiplike tail called a flagellum.

The tsetse fly carries this dangerous parasite. In some African languages, *tsetse* (teet-SEE) means "fly." It is a nasty critter. Larger than a horsefly and extremely aggressive, it is brown in color, with bulging eyes and a great pointed snout. Victims describe its bite as a red-hot needle jabbing into their skin. Male and female tsetses feed only on blood. In doing so, they also take in

The head of a tsetse fly showing its biting apparatus.

immature trypanosomes from infected persons and animals. The parasites reach adulthood in the fly's stomach, then pass to the next person or animal the tsetse bites. Once inside a new host, the trypanosomes reproduce in its bloodstream, eventually settling in the nervous system, particularly the brain.

Most cases of sleeping sickness start with symptoms like those of the common cold: fever, headache, chills. Doctors detect the disease with blood samples that show the parasites under a microscope. They treat it with drugs containing arsenic, a powerful poison, and deadly if not used in the correct dose. If treatment starts before trypanosomes enter the brain, the victim will almost surely recover. If not treated early, the victim sleeps for ever-longer periods, finally slipping into a coma ending in death. The best way to deal with sleeping sickness is to stop the trypanosomes before they enter a human host. Recently, African countries aided by the World Health Organization (WHO) have begun campaigns to eradicate the tsetse fly. They do this by burning any brush the insects live in and by large-scale spraying of insecticides. Even so, the WHO estimates that between 300,000 and 500,000 people are affected by sleeping sickness.

Deadly as they are, the parasites carried by tsetse flies do not compare with those of other insects. Due to their parasites, several insect species are the most dangerous creatures that have ever existed. Over the centuries, mosquitoes, fleas, and lice have transmitted diseases that killed hundreds of millions of people. Those diseases have determined the outcome of wars, even shaped the course of history. Because of their importance, they demand chapters of their own.

The malaria germ does not go into the mosquito for nothing. . . . It is there for a purpose and that purpose . . . is its own interests—germs are selfish brutes.
— **PATRICK MANSON**, physician, to Ronald Ross, awarded the Nobel Prize in 1902 for discovery of the life cycle of the malarial parasite, in 1897

4 Mosquitoes and Selfish Brutes

Writers Andrew Spielman and Michael D'Antonio titled their marvelous book *Mosquito: The Story of Man's Deadliest Foe*. It is a good title, because no creature has ever brought more misery to humanity than these winged parasites and the even smaller parasites—"selfish brutes"—they transmit.

Mosquitoes are flies; the word is Spanish for "little fly." Like all flies, they have two wings. Most species are less than a quarter-inch long, the size of a baby's eyelash, and just about as heavy. Yet

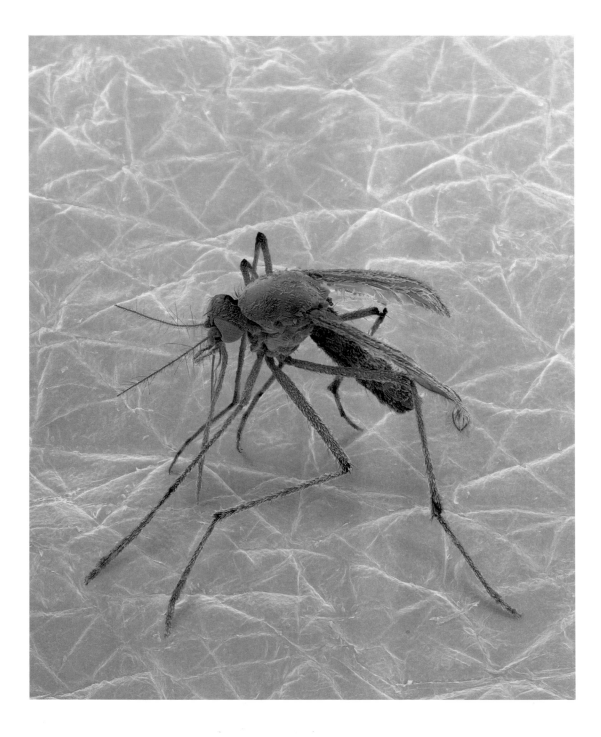

they have not always been so little. The earliest mosquitoes known to science lived 144 million years ago, the very time in which the dinosaurs reached their greatest size. Preserved in amber, a type of fossilized pine tree sap, some ancient mosquitoes were four times larger than their modern relatives, and probably much noisier. A mosquito's wings move about 1,000 times a second, creating the dreaded humming sound. An ancient mosquito must have sounded like an electric razor.

There are over 2,700 species of mosquitoes throughout the world today. These live everywhere from tropical jungles to the vast, treeless Arctic wastelands. Mosquitoes have also been found at elevations of 14,000 feet in the mountains of India and at depths of nearly 4,000 feet in South African gold mines. About 150 species live in the United States.

Although most people regard them as pests, mosquitoes play an important part in the natural order. Birds, fish, frogs, spiders, dragonflies, and other insects depend on them as a source of food. Like bees and wasps, mosquitoes pollinate flowers and plants eaten by other creatures. Most species are harmless, spending their adulthood sipping nectar and plant juices. Very few species take blood, and among these only the female does. She has no choice, because she must have certain chemicals found in blood to produce fertile eggs. Without those chemicals, blood-taking

Poised for action, a female mosquito stands above a blood vessel ready to "bite."

mosquitoes would disappear. The females of different species prefer the blood of different animal hosts. Some only suck the blood of frogs, snakes, turtles, or lizards. Others take blood from birds and mammals, including humans.

Life Cycle of a Parasite: DIRECT

Different parasites have different life cycles. The term life cycle refers to the stages an organism must pass through to reach adulthood. If it has a direct life cycle, a young parasite infects the same host, or the same type of host, it came from. An adult female worm, let's say, may live in a dog's or cat's intestines, where it lays eggs. After the eggs pass out in the host's feces, the same or another dog or cat may lick them up. The eggs then hatch and grow to adulthood inside the host, repeating the cycle.

Bloodsucking insects are marvels of design. The female mosquito uses various methods to solve key problems. First, she must locate her prey. To do this, she has an array of delicate sensors. Chemical sensors in the two antennae placed between her eyes detect carbon dioxide, a gas breathed out by birds and mammals, up to 100 feet away. As she flies closer, the two large eyes covering most of her head go into action. These are very different from the eyes of animals with backbones. Our eyes are able to focus on an object to create a sharp image. Mosquitoes and other insects have "compound eyes." This means that each eye has thousands of six-sided lenses, placed at different angles and working independently of each other. While a mosquito's eyes cannot see an image clearly, they can detect the slightest movement. On a female's final approach, heat sensors in her antennae zero in on a blood vessel.

Second, a female mosquito must take blood quickly. She cannot bite, for she has no teeth or jaws, as leeches and lions do. Instead, she pierces her victim's skin and sucks blood with a set of mouthparts nested inside a groove running down the center of her long proboscis. Among these mouthparts are twin pairs of thin, saw-toothed blades called stylets.

Let's say a female mosquito lands on your arm. If you watch her with a magnifying glass, you would see that she does not plunge her entire proboscis into your flesh like an injection

Life Cycle of a Parasite: INDIRECT

If it has an indirect life cycle, a young parasite must pass through a different type of host, or "vector," before it can infect its final host. A vector is an organism that carries a parasite from one host to another without knowing it or intending to.

There are two ways a vector can carry a parasite to its host: First, vectors may inject young parasites directly into the final host. Second, the host may swallow the infected vector while feeding normally. Once inside the host, however, the parasite completes its life cycle, maturing into an adult.

Mosquitoes are examples of the first method, because they carry and inject the parasite that causes malaria into the bloodstream of other birds and animals. Various types of parasitic worms find their final hosts using the second method. So, for example, by swallowing water with tiny shrimplike sea creatures living in it, animals can be infected by the parasitic young worms living inside the tiny creatures.

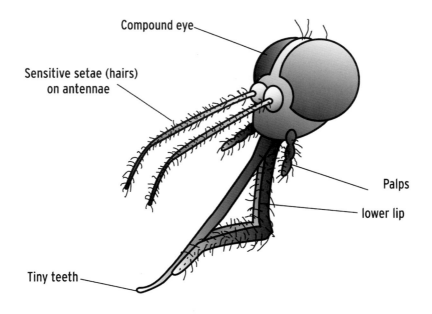

Compound eye

Sensitive setae (hairs)
on antennae

Palps

lower lip

Tiny teeth

Diagram of a mosquito head

needle. Instead, the proboscis bends to allow the stylets to slip out of their groove and cut into your flesh with quick back-and-forth strokes. Once they are inside, sensors on the stylets find a capillary, a blood vessel so tiny that only a single red blood cell can pass through it at a time. Instantly, twin tubes near the stylets slip into the opening. One tube dribbles a chemical similar to the leech's herudin to prevent the blood from clotting; the other tube sucks blood into her belly. Having taken her fill, she flies away after two or three minutes, her stomach heavy and swollen with blood. A nerve in her stomach senses when she is full. Should the nerve get damaged, she would keep sucking blood, and keep swelling, until she bursts apart. Since most people are allergic to the clot-preventing chemical, an itchy bump forms on the skin. We call that bump a "mosquito bite."

Female mosquitoes lay their eggs wherever they can find still water: lakes, ponds, marshes, tin cans, hollow tree trunks, and discarded tires. The eggs hatch into larvae. Hanging head down in the water, each larva or "wriggler" has a breathing tube at the rear end of its body, which it pushes above the surface of the water, into the air. After a few days, the larva becomes inactive and forms a pupa, later emerging as a winged adult. Most adult mosquitoes, males and females, live just two to three weeks.

Mosquitoes have been (and still are) responsible for more human deaths than any other creature that has ever existed. This is because the females of bloodsucking species have their own parasites, which they transmit while feeding. Some of these parasites are viruses. In humans, mosquito-borne viruses cause diseases such as yellow fever, dengue (DEHN-gay) fever, and encephalitis (ehn-sehf-uh-LY-tihs), or swelling of the brain.

Other mosquito parasites are *protozoa*, single-celled organisms that spend part of their life cycle inside their winged host and the other part inside the animals female mosquitoes take blood from. The chief mosquito-borne protozoa belong to the genus *Plasmodium*. Of this genus's more than 175 named members, most infect a wide range of animals. In each case, the protozoa cause

Mosquito larvae hanging head-down, their breathing tubes pushing through the surface to get air.

a disease called malaria. Those affected include birds, bats, rats, mice, porcupines, squirrels, lizards, snakes, turtles, and monkeys. Animal forms of malaria do not usually kill; hosts manage to live with the infection or throw it off entirely.

Human malaria is different. Four species of the *Plasmodium* parasite infect people. Of these, three cause mild infections, so the victim usually recovers with little or any permanent harm. But the fourth species, *Plasmodium falciparum*, is a mass murderer, by far the deadliest human parasite ever. No disease, including plague and smallpox, can match its grim record. *Plasmodium falciparum* has killed more people than all wars, famines, and natural disasters combined.

Today malaria is a major public health problem in over 90 countries. It is also the leading cause of death across the globe. The U.S. Centers for Disease Control and Prevention estimate that no fewer than 300 million people have malaria, whether in its most deadly or milder forms. Of those it has infected, malaria kills between 1.5 and 2.7 million people per year. The infection is especially dangerous for young people, taking the lives of 3,000 children under five every day, or one child every 30 seconds, mostly in Africa. Mere numbers, however, cannot express its toll in human pain and suffering.

Little more than a century ago, nobody knew what caused malaria or how it spread. *Mala aria* means "bad air" in Italian. Since ancient times, people believed the infection came from rotting marsh plants. Supposedly, you got sick by breathing the putrid air, or the air surrounding an infected person. But this is not so. In the nineteenth century, the real cause of malaria was revealed.

Those who finally discovered the truth about malaria had certain things in common. All had boundless curiosity and a stubborn streak that made them keep going despite setbacks. More, the pursuit for the cure showed that people of goodwill, even in rival nations, can build on one another's work for the good of humanity.

Dr. Charles-Louis-Alphonse Laveran.

A French army doctor made the first breakthrough. Charles-Louis-Alphonse Laveran (1845–1922) had studied with Louis Pasteur in Paris. The great scientist's achievements and example inspired Laveran. In 1880, while posted to a French military hospital in North Africa, he identified *Plasmodium falciparum* in red blood cells taken from an infected soldier. For weeks on end, in the stifling heat, Laveran studied blood samples from other malaria patients under his microscope. All had the exact same protozoan. Clearly, he decided, it caused the disease. Yet Laveran could not show *how* the killer got into its victims in the first place.

Ronald Ross (1857–1932) took the next step. He was born in India, which was then governed by Great Britain. Ross's parents sent him to England as a teenager to finish his education. He earned a medical degree and became an army doctor upon returning to India. Ross spent much of his time tending to malaria patients, but with little success. Most died. Since malaria killed so many each year, Indians called it the "King of Diseases."

An incident sparked Ross's interest in mosquitoes as possible carriers of the *Plasmodium* parasite. The insects always buzzed around his barracks. A particularly large swarm, he noticed, seemed to favor a water barrel kept outside his window in case of fire. Looking inside, he saw swarms of mosquito larvae wriggling to and fro. Ross tipped the barrel over, emptying it. Sure enough, within days his quarters were nearly mosquito-free. When he asked the post commander to order all water barrels covered or emptied,

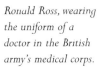

Ronald Ross, wearing the uniform of a doctor in the British army's medical corps.

he got a scolding. "Much to my surprise," Ross later recalled, "he was very scornful." Why? Because getting rid of mosquitoes "would be unsettling to the order of nature, as mosquitoes were created for some purpose [and] it was our duty to bear with them!" Ross disagreed. Mosquitoes were pests. Perhaps they might also have something to do with malaria. He decided to find out.

Ross captured any mosquitoes he could find. Then he let the females loose on malaria patients who had volunteered as human guinea pigs. The insects refused to feed.

After months of failure, it dawned on Ross that he might be using the wrong species of mosquitoes. One day, a servant captured adult mosquitoes of a type he had never seen before. Ross called them "dappled-wings," because they had dark spots, or "dapples," on their wings. These belonged to the genus *Anopheles*. Of the 450 species of *Anopheles*, we now know that some 50 species transmit the malaria parasite.

The doctor turned to his microscope. Ross began with an *Anopheles* mosquito in a test tube, one that had fed on a malaria patient. After killing it with a puff of cigar smoke, he placed it on a glass slide. Holding it steady with a pair of forceps, he opened it with the point of a needle. The work went slowly, for the mosquito's stomach was so tiny that he might easily have torn it to shreds. After a while, Ross saw strangely colored cells in the stomach wall. Before he could investigate further, the army sent him to the city of Calcutta. The winter of 1898 was very cold, so Ross had hardly any human malaria patients to study. Instead, he turned to the next best thing: bird malaria.

These studies showed that the *Anopheles* mosquitoes Ross allowed to feed on infected sparrows got the malaria parasite, then passed it to uninfected sparrows. This convinced him that the disease must follow the same course in humans as in birds. That was enough for Ross; he ended his research without taking the final step. An Italian biology professor, Giovanni Battista Grassi (1854–1925), did the rest. In 1899, Grassi proved that human malaria goes through the same life cycle as bird malaria, and that only female *Anopheles* mosquitoes transmit the parasite to people.

Later scientists completed the picture of malaria. Now all agree that Africa is the mother continent of the malaria parasite, and of the human race. Both originated there more than a million years ago.

Giovanni Battista Grassi.

About 50,000 years ago, small bands of hunters began to leave Africa, heading northward and eastward in search of better hunting grounds in Europe and Asia. Members of some bands carried the malaria parasite in their bodies. Had these hunters moved into lands without *Anopheles* mosquitoes, the victims of malaria among them would have died off and the parasite would not have spread. However, since *Anopheles* mosquitoes live on every continent, the infection spread, passing from person to mosquito to person down the generations. In the early 1500s, it came to the New World aboard ships carrying European

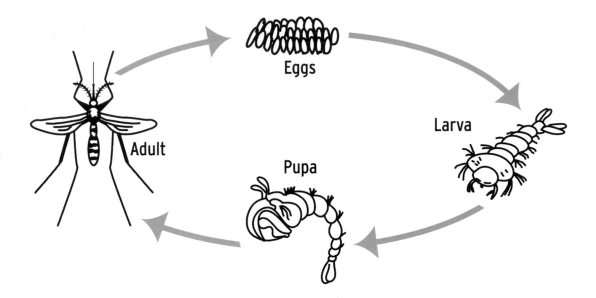

Eggs

Larva

Adult

Pupa

*Mosquito
life cycle*

immigrants and African slaves. Within three centuries, malaria spread across the United States, even into Canada.

The malaria parasite, we know, has a three-stage life cycle. In its first stage, a female *Anopheles* mosquito gets the immature parasites in blood from an infected person. After maturing in the mosquito's stomach, the adult parasites move into her salivary glands.

In the second stage, if the mosquito feeds on an uninfected person, the adult parasites travel through the bloodstream to the newly infected person's liver. There, each adult parasite divides into thousands of "daughter cells." Normally, these kinds of invaders would trigger the host's immune system, designed to detect and destroy foreign bodies. Yet *Plasmodium falciparum* daughter cells do nothing of the sort. Instead, they act like spaceships in science-fiction stories that switch on "cloaking" devices to make themselves invisible. Each daughter cell releases chemicals that hide it from the immune system, or fool the system into treating the invader as part of the host's body.

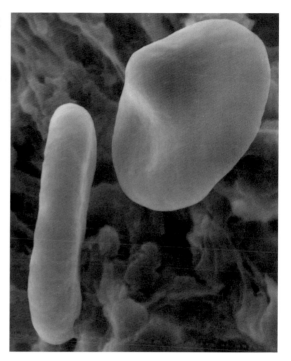

A misshaped red blood cell infected by malaria daughter cells.

The daughter cells soon leave the liver and find their way into the bloodstream. Each drop of blood has millions of red blood cells containing the chemical hemoglobin. This chemical enables red blood cells to collect oxygen in the lungs and deliver it throughout the body by way of the bloodstream. When malaria daughter cells invade red blood cells, they digest the hemoglobin, multiplying further while killing the cells. The dead cells burst, releasing more parasites to invade more red blood cells, and so on. Finally, another mosquito bites the infected person and the parasites complete their life cycle in her stomach.

Meanwhile, the infected person feels the full effects of malaria. Shaking chills, high fever, and severe muscle aches occur each time the parasites burst out of red blood cells. Millions of them break out at once. A shortage of healthy red cells causes anemia, a condition that deprives the body of the oxygen it needs to work properly. Heart, lungs, and brain begin to fail, bringing death.

Malaria has left its mark on history. Mighty warriors clad in armor have fallen to the microscopic *Plasmodium falciparum*. In 323 B.C., while marching to India, Alexander the Great died of malaria just as he seemed about to conquer the entire known world. Since then, the disease has ravaged cities and entire regions across the globe. Malaria, an equal-opportunity killer, has felled popes and princes, kings and emperors, geniuses and fools. Eight presidents of the United States suffered from malaria but survived: George Washington, James Monroe, Andrew Jackson, Abraham Lincoln, Ulysses S. Grant, James A. Garfield, Theodore Roosevelt, and John F. Kennedy.

In ancient times, the Roman Empire collapsed partly because of malaria. Rome's experience is a marvelous example of how humans can spread disease by abusing the natural environment. About 2,000 years ago, the Romans chopped down the forests that covered the hills around their city for building materials and firewood. With the forests gone, the land could not drain properly after rainstorms. Instead of being absorbed by the trees' roots, water collected on the ground. Marshes formed. *Anopheles* mosquitoes, always present in Italy, flourished—and with them *Plasmodium falciparum* parasites carried from Africa in the bodies of slaves.

For centuries, the city of Rome was the malaria capital of the world. Terrified citizens built temples to the Goddess of Fever, an ugly monster-woman, sacrificing to her in the hope

A child representing the New World gives the gift of quinine to an adult representing Europe.

that she would spare them. Malaria caused a steep drop in population, especially among the young. In 2001, scientists found a cemetery holding the skeletons of scores of newborn babies in earthen jars. Tests showed that nearly all had died of malaria more than a thousand years ago.

In modern times, quinine was the first effective malaria remedy. This bitter-tasting drug comes from the bark of cinchona (sihn-KOH-nuh), a type of evergreen tree that grows on the slopes of the Andes Mountains in South America. The native peoples of Peru and Ecuador had long used quinine to treat fevers of all sorts. During the 1600s, Spanish priests sent to the New World to convert the Indians to Christianity sent quinine samples home. When doctors gave the drug to malaria sufferers, they recovered, though nobody could explain why. Today we know that quinine changes the hemoglobin in infected red blood cells to a poison that kills the malaria parasite but is harmless to humans.

Spain governed much of South America in the 1600s, and after. To keep the price of quinine high, it banned the growing of cinchona except in its own colonies. Thus, there was never enough of the precious drug to go around, and prices rose sky-high. In 1861, English traders took matters into their own hands by stealing some cinchona seeds. These they sold to Dutch businessmen, who planted them on Java, a Dutch island colony in the Indian Ocean. Even so, planters could not grow enough quinine to meet world needs. That changed during World War II. From 1941 to 1945, Japanese forces occupied Java. With their chief source of quinine in enemy hands, American and British chemists found quinine substitutes. These chemicals not only prevent the malaria parasite from taking hold in the human body, but also cure the disease.

Having learned malaria's cause and how it spreads, it became possible for scientists to fight the disease on a large scale. In the 1950s and 1960s, govern- ments attacked *Plasmodium falciparum* by spraying chemical insecticides, drain- ing marshes where *Anopheles* mosqui- toes bred, and spreading oil on water to suffocate their larvae.

Yet the *Anopheles* mosquito and the *Plasmodium* parasite still exist, even in the world's wealthiest countries. Some progress has been made. For example, in 1947 the United States government reported 15,000 cases of malaria, but in 2002 only 1,337 cases, including eight deaths. Africa, where malaria began, is still its stronghold. Malaria kills as many as 800,000 children a year in Africa. Thus, humanity has not won its war against malaria—not by a long shot.

Caught in the act! Malaria daughter cells breaking out of a red blood cell.

There are several reasons for malaria's survival. One is money. Poor countries lack the funds to buy antimalarial drugs. Nor can they easily afford nets treated with insecticide to protect people from mosquitoes while asleep at night. Friendly governments, wealthy individuals, and the World Health Organization give some help, saving countless lives. Still, helpers face long odds.

Fighting malaria has become a race against time. It is a race in which humans must run faster and faster just to stay where they are. This is partly because *Anopheles* mosquitoes are born survivors. While insecticides kill countless mosquitoes, they never kill them all. The survivors then pass their genes to the next generation, along with immunity to certain insecticides. Thus, scientists must always seek new chemicals to overcome the mosquitoes' newly gained immunity. Yet these new chemicals may have unpleasant, perhaps even dangerous side effects of their own.

It is the same with *Plasmodium falciparum*. Like mosquitoes and insecticides, sooner or later these protozoa will develop resistance to the drugs in use today.

Global warming, the gradual rise in temperatures across our planet, threatens humanity in a special way. Some scientists believe the temperature rise noted over the last century is as normal and natural as the global cooling that happened earlier in our Earth's history. Other scientists think people are causing global warming. They say the gases released by human inventions such as automobile engines and coal-burning power plants trap heat in the atmosphere, causing temperatures to rise. Global warming carries health dangers, whatever its cause. Warming can change weather patterns, bringing more humidity, rainfall, and flooding. These in turn could lead to an increase in mosquitoes of all species. Increasing the range of malaria-bearing *Anopheles* mosquitoes would spread malaria farther, into new regions. Thus, *Plasmodium falciparum* may be on the verge of an outbreak that will threaten humanity as never before.

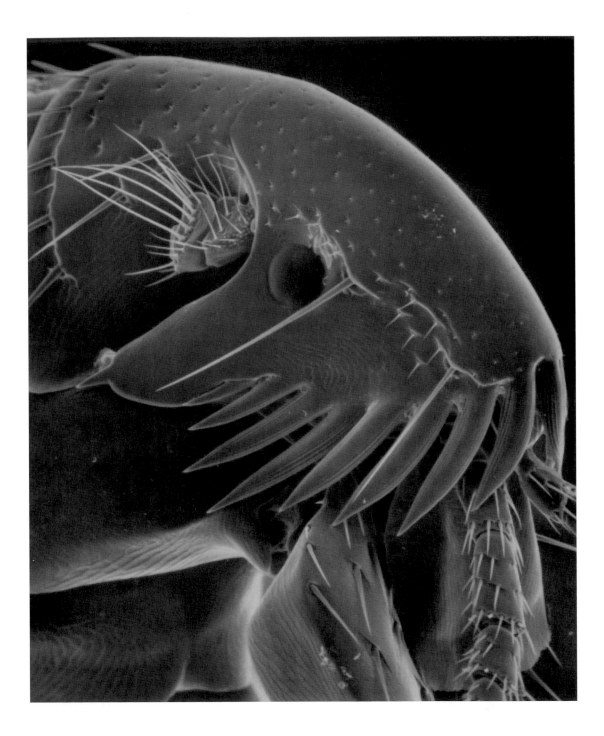

5 Fearsome Fleas

FLEAS

Anton van Leeuwenhoek was the first to study fleas closely. Since his time, scientists have discovered over 2,380 flea species worldwide. A fossil flea recently found in Australia dates from the era of the dinosaurs. It is about 200 million years old, yet it appears not to differ from modern fleas in any important way.

Fleas are reddish-brown, wingless insects that range from one-sixteenth to one-eighth of an inch in length. Their genus name, *Siphonaptera*, tells a lot about them. *Siphonaptera* is Greek for a wingless creature with a siphon; that is, a tube for sucking

The fearsome cat flea. Protected by the "armor" plates of its external skeleton, the flea can fall from the top of a building and survive.

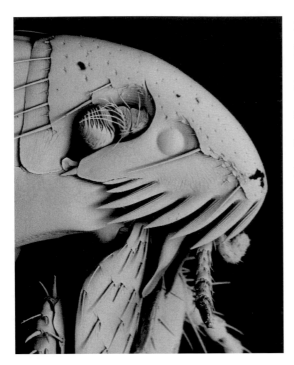

The head of a flea. Notice the round eye in the center.

fluids. All fleas, male and female, are bloodsucking ectoparasites of mammals and birds. Scientists name each species for its favorite host: cat flea, dog flea, rabbit flea, penguin flea, horse flea, human flea, and so on.

The flea is a champion of survival. Everything about it is designed to increase its chances of success in a dangerous world. Protected by the "armor" plates of its external skeleton, the flea is shock-resistant. It can fall from the top of a building, land safely, and jump away as if nothing happened. With its tiny head, body flattened vertically like a sunfish, and stiff, backward-pointing hairs, the flea can move easily through the hairs or feathers of its host. Should you catch a flea, you will find it impossible to crush between your fingers; it will just slip out. Monkeys crush fleas between their teeth.

Fleas are very strong, particularly when it comes to jumping ability. Although they are unable to fly, powerful hind legs allow them to leap great distances. For example, the human-body flea can jump 13 inches, or 104 times its own body length. In human terms, that would mean a child four feet tall could jump 416 feet—more than the length of a football field!

Although adult fleas live on the skin of other creatures, females lay their eggs in their hosts' nests or homes. Newly hatched flea larvae feed on the hosts' shed skin cells and any other debris they find, including their parents' feces. When they become adults, the fleas seek a host and start sucking its blood. Both sexes get their nourishment from blood. Females also need blood to produce fertile eggs, laying from four to forty eggs a day.

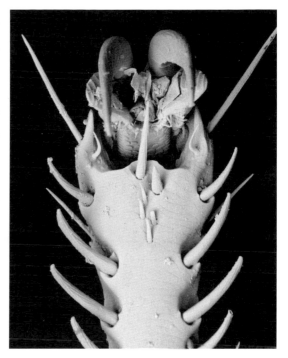

The siphon, or piercing-sucking mouthpart, of a flea.

Fleas have always fascinated people. In the 1600s, European royalty kept them as pets. As a child, King Louis XIV of France had a tiny set of gold cannons drawn by fleas with thin golden wires tied around their necks. In "The Flea," English poet John Donne honored the insect that had bitten him and his lady love, mingling their blood and thus joining them together forever. Famed for cruelty, Queen Christina of Sweden amused herself by executing fleas with a miniature cannon made for that purpose alone. In the 1700s, wealthy Mexican women spent their

Fleas dressed up.

idle hours dressing dead fleas in colorful costumes made of velvet and lace.

Before movies and television, flea circuses toured the cities of Europe and America. These circuses featured troupes of fleas "trained" to do amazing tricks. Yet the tricks were a hoax based on cruelty. For example, when trainers put caustic chemicals on lightweight balls, the fleas kicked them away, making it seem as if they were playing soccer. Sometimes circuses featured "flea orchestras." A trainer would glue live fleas to a metal dish and then glue tiny musical instruments to the fleas. When he heated the dish, the insects struggled to escape, giving the impression that they were playing the instruments.

There is nothing amusing about the harm caused to people by fleas. Chemicals in a flea's saliva may trigger strong allergic reactions in bite victims. Fleas, in turn, have parasites of their own, including various mites. A single flea was found carrying 150 mites of the same species, some of which may be harmful to humans. Fleas are also hosts to tapeworms, protozoa, and bacteria.

Living in dirty conditions, as many people did during the Middle Ages, allows disease-carrying creatures like fleas to feed, breed, and thrive. Fleas are most dangerous to people as parasites of rats. The black rat, *Rattus rattus*, used to be common in Asia and Europe. Black rats like to stay close to their nests, a habit that made them cozy in the houses most Europeans lived in centuries ago. These houses, jammed close together along narrow unpaved streets, were little more than leaky wooden boxes with straw roofs and mud floors. During the dry season, the wind kicked up dust storms in the streets. Rains turned the streets into rivers of mud. These filthy streets were wonderful places for rats and their fleas.

Lacking sanitation services, townspeople threw garbage and bodily wastes out their windows. To protect pedestrians from showers of filth, laws required citizens to give warning by crying "Look out below!" Toilet paper, a modern invention, did not exist. Instead, people wiped themselves with straw, hay, or curved sticks. Citizens named streets for human wastes. Paris, for example, had the rue du Pipi (Urine Street) and the rue Merdeux (Dung Street). Palaces were no cleaner than the homes of ordinary folks. In the Louvre, the French royal palace, nobles relieved themselves on the marble floors, behind pillars, and under the stairways. The palace smelled like a sewer.

Pigs were the only form of public sanitation. Most townspeople had pigs as a source of cheap food. They kept the porkers in outdoor sheds, or in their homes; squealing pigs made good burglar alarms. During the day, owners let their pigs roam the streets, eating trash. Sometimes pigs became wild, terrorizing pedestrians and invading homes. When this happened, the pig was killed and its owner charged for the return of its body.

Most Europeans, including royalty, seldom (if ever) bathed or washed their hands after relieving themselves. Born in 1347, Saint Catherine of Siena, in northern Italy, never bathed. King Louis XIV had two baths in his life: the first at his baptism, the second on doctor's orders after a minor operation. Queen Christina joked that she did not know the color of her hands "because they were too foul"; she never washed them. The wealthy doused their bodies with perfume, invented to mask foul odors. Ordinary folks just stank to high heaven.

Clothes swarmed with vermin—various small pests— so people scratched constantly. For example, in 1170, while preparing the body of Saint Thomas à Becket for burial, English priests discovered that the holy man wore eight layers of clothing. Upon removing the final layer, a priest noted, "the vermin boiled over like water in a simmering cauldron." Saint Francis of Assisi thought putting up with biting fleas made him more humble, bringing him closer to God. He called fleas "the pearls of poverty," and never killed even one. Women often wore around their necks ornate flea traps, long metal tubes with holes, lined inside with sticky paper. Some women held small dogs on their laps as living flea traps, drawing insects to themselves and away from their owners. We still call small pet dogs "lapdogs."

Plague

Black rats were most common during the Middle Ages because of the cramped, dirty conditions of towns and cities. Like all rats, they have parasites, particularly *Xenopsylla cheopis*, the black

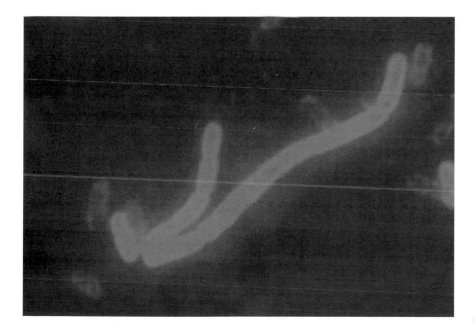

Yersinia pestis, *the bacterium that causes plague.*

rat flea. As we have seen, fleas have parasites, too. One parasite is the bacillus, or rod-shaped bacterium, *Yersinia pestis*, Latin for "Yersin's pest." As used here, *pest* means more than a nuisance, or something that annoys us. Originally, it was a term for plague. The bacterium is named for Alexandre Yersin, who discovered that it caused plague. We will meet the famous scientist soon.

Like all bacteria, *Yersinia pestis* reproduces by dividing into two identical individuals. These new bacteria divide so often and so quickly that they form a blockage preventing a flea's blood meal from reaching its stomach. Wild with hunger, the insect bites the rat's skin repeatedly. Unable to get blood past the blockage, the flea spits bacteria-filled saliva into the wound, thus infecting the rat.

Like all warm-blooded animals', a rat's body cools when it dies. Fleas hate cold, so they leave the body and leap onto another, healthy rat. Here is the problem. If they cannot find another rat, they leap onto a person. The hungry insects bite their new host, injecting them with plague bacteria. Yet the fleas, like the rat, are doomed. Still unable to satisfy their hunger, they die. But not before passing the infection to a human host.

Symptoms of plague soon appear. Within days of being bitten, lymph nodes (glands) in the infected person's legs, neck, armpits, and groin swell to the size of hens' eggs. People used to call these painful swellings buboes—from *bubon*, the Greek word for groin. That is why the disease was named bubonic plague.

When swollen buboes break open, sticky foul-smelling pus oozes out. Other symptoms include high fever, stabbing headaches, muscle aches, and general weakness. If the fever breaks by the tenth day, it means the victim's immune system has won the battle for life, destroying the bacteria. If the fever does not break, the toxins (poisons) released by the bacteria bring death. One out of two bubonic plague victims always died. Before death, blood vessels burst and leaked under the skin, forming a black bruise. Thus, bubonic plague's other name, *Black Death*.

Bubonic plague is the most common form of *Yersinia pestis*. Two other forms are even deadlier. In the first form, *Yersinia pestis* may directly infect the bloodstream, racing throughout the body to cause blood poisoning. In the second form, *Yersinia pestis* may get into the lungs. Victims then easily give the infection to others by coughing and sneezing bacteria in a fine spray. In either case, the disease kills all victims within hours, not days, of their becoming infected.

In 1347, the worst outbreak of bubonic plague ever recorded began in China. Within the year, it reached Italy in the holds of rat-infested merchant ships. What people at the time called the "Great Dying" then raced along the trade routes to every country in Western Europe.

Nobody had ever seen anything like the Great Dying before. Totally ignorant of its cause, people became terrified, confused, and panicky. With dead bodies sprawled everywhere, even in the streets, the social order began to break down. Love and friendship, honor and duty, no longer bound people to one another. Agnolo di Tura, of Siena, Italy, survived to write about his experiences.

It was a cruel and horrible thing . . . and it is impossible for the human tongue to recount the awful truth. . . . The victims died almost immediately. They would swell beneath their armpits and in their groins, and fall over dead while talking. Father abandoned child, wife husband, one brother another. . . . And so they died. . . . And they died by the hundreds, both day and night. . . . And I, Agnolo di Tura, called the Fat, buried my five children with my own hands. And so many died that all believed it was the end of the world. And no medicine or any other defense availed.

Doctors tried anything they could think of to prevent or cure plague. To protect themselves while visiting patients, they wore robes with pointed hoods, long gloves, high boots, and a mask shaped liked a crow's head. Placing pungent herbs and spices in the mask's "beak," they hoped, would fend off the infection.

Many Europeans believed God sent plague as punishment for their sins. Begging His forgiveness, some men deliberately hurt themselves to save others. Called flagellants, from the Latin word for whip, they marched in groups thousands strong, billowing purple banners embroidered with golden crosses behind them. Before joining a band, a man vowed not to wash, shave, sleep in a bed, or change clothes while the epidemic lasted.

A doctor visiting plague victims wearing his beaked mask.

Upon reaching a town, the entire band stripped to the waist and formed a circle. Each man held a whip made of strips of knotted leather tipped with iron spikes. Chanting prayers, the band slowly walked in a circle, each man striking his chest and the back of the man in front. The band kept walking, whipping, and chanting prayers of forgiveness. Blood streamed down men's bodies, leaving red trails on the ground. Sometimes spikes stuck in the skin and had to be wrenched out, tearing away chunks of flesh.

Flagellants visited the hometown of the French historian and poet Jean Froissart. According to Froissart's *Chronicles*,

Flagellants visiting a French town during the Great Dying.

written about 1369, all the townspeople watched the visitors, trembling, weeping, and groaning in sympathy.

> *Some men made themselves bleed very badly between the shoulder blades and some foolish women had cloths ready to catch the blood and smear it on their eyes, saying it was miraculous blood. When they were doing penance, they sang very mournful songs about the nativity and passion of Our Lord. The object of this penance was to entreat [beg] God to put a stop to the mortality. For in that time of plague . . . people died suddenly and at least a third of all the people in the world died.*

Eventually, the epidemic burned itself out for reasons scientists still do not entirely understand. Yet the flagellants had nothing to do with that. If anything, plague often broke out after they left a town, because they had infected fleas on their skin and clothing.

Modern historians believe that between 1348 and 1351, plague killed one in three Europeans. Thus, out of a population of around 75 million, roughly 25 million died within those three awful years. However, plague never entirely disappeared; it tormented Europe for another four centuries. Less severe than the first outbreak, it visited different places at different times. Finally, by the 1800s, advances in sanitation and hygiene helped control rats in Europe and America. Poorer countries in Asia and the Middle East continued to suffer outbreaks.

In 1894, another major epidemic began in China and India. Within six years, plague claimed 12 million lives. By then, however, science had made great strides. At last, scientific detectives discovered what caused the disease and how it spread.

Dr. Alexandre Yersin (1863–1943) was born in Switzerland but eventually became a French citizen. Although a trained physician, Yersin preferred medical research to treating patients. In 1886, he became a student of Louis Pasteur's, the greatest

Dr. Alexandre Yersin

researcher of the day. When plague broke out in Hong Kong, a territory on the Chinese coast governed by Great Britain, Pasteur asked Yersin to find its cause.

Upon his arrival in Hong Kong, Yersin ran into an unexpected problem. It had nothing to do with plague, as there was no shortage of victims to study. The problem was that Dr. James A. Lowson, the British medical chief, hated French people and anyone who worked with them. Lowson refused to let Yersin study plague victims' bodies in the hospital morgue.

A stubborn man, Yersin refused to take no for an answer. He built a tiny hut near the hospital, equipping it with a folding cot, a microscope, glass slides, and test tubes. One night, he bribed two hospital workers to let him into the morgue for a few minutes. While they stood guard at the door, Yersin "stole" pus from the buboes of a patient who had just died of plague.

He made a breakthrough discovery at once. Seeing rod-shaped bacteria in the pus samples, Yersin reasoned that they caused plague. To test his idea, he injected pus into healthy guinea pigs.

All died of plague. Sure enough, when Yersin dissected the guinea pigs, he found their blood teeming with the rod-shaped bacteria. Next, Yersin examined the bodies of hundreds of dead rats found in the streets. They also teemed with bacteria identical to those found in the bodies of plague victims. Clearly, then, the same species of bacteria that caused plague in rats also caused it in humans. In Yersin's honor, fellow scientists named the bacteria *Yersinia*

Dr. Paul-Louis Simond administering an injection.

pestis. Yet a question still remained. How did the bacteria get into each host in the first place?

Another student of Pasteur's answered that question. In 1897, Dr. Paul-Louis Simond (1858–1947) visited the French colony of Indochina, today's Republic of Vietnam. There he noticed that people living in houses blocks away from where plague had struck often came down with plague, too. Simond asked victims what they had done in the days before getting sick. Some said they had picked up dead rats by their tails before tossing them into the gutter.

Simond decided to play a hunch. Knowing that fleas left

infected rats when their bodies cooled, he captured several from a rat that had just died. He did it by pushing them into a test tube with his bare hands, a brave act, but a foolish one. When Simond dissected the fleas under his microscope, he found them teeming with plague bacteria.

Next, Simond built a glass cage with two "rooms" separated by a mesh screen just wide enough for a flea to squeeze through. In one cage he placed a plague-infected rat, in the other a healthy rat. The rats had no contact with each other. Yet the healthy rat died of plague when infected fleas leaped onto it after the sick rat died. Simond would always remember how he felt that day. "I was," he wrote in his diary, "deeply moved with the inexpressible feeling of having just betrayed a secret which had scared mankind since the early days of plague in the world."

The twin discoveries of what caused plague and how it spread held the key to fighting the disease. Governments began massive sanitation programs to eliminate garbage and the rats that fed on it. Insecticides destroyed fleas. Blood tests detected *Yersinia pestis* in a victim's body before the infection took hold. Antibiotics killed the bacteria.

Despite these advances, plague is still with us. Parts of East Africa, South America, Vietnam, and Hunan province in China constantly have minor outbreaks of the disease. Every year, the

World Health Organization reports between 1,000 and 3,000 cases of plague globally. Fortunately, antibiotics save most victims' lives.

Nor is the United States immune from plague. In 1924, the last serious outbreak struck Los Angeles, California. *Yersinia pestis* had come ashore in rats and infected fleas aboard cargo ships from the Far East. Since then, researchers have found *Yersinia pestis* in wild rodents in most western states, especially ground squirrels and prairie dogs. Some national parks have signs warning visitors to stay away from these rodents. From 1980 to 1994, the United States Centers for Disease Control reported 229 cases of plague, with 33 deaths; two others died in 1996.

Here is something else to think about. Plague has a long history as a weapon of war. A year before the epidemic of 1348 started, an attacking army flung the bodies of plague victims into Kaffa, a port on the Black Sea, causing an outbreak. In 1422, Russian troops tried to spread plague among their Swedish enemies by leaving the bodies of plague victims near their camps. Finally, during World War II, Japanese researchers turned plague into a true biological weapon. In secret laboratories, they bred millions of plague-infected fleas. Japanese aircraft then dropped the fleas over China; the resulting epidemic killed thousands of civilians. The Japanese military also planned to use infected fleas against American forces fighting in the Pacific. Luckily, a U.S. submarine sank the ship that carried both the infected fleas and a team of biological warfare experts.

Scientists today believe that bubonic plague could also be used as a terrorist weapon. Bioterrorism emerged in the United States after terrorists crashed airliners into the World Trade Center and the Pentagon on September 11, 2001. Within weeks of these disasters, five Americans died of anthrax sent in letters through the mail. Anthrax is an animal disease that can strike humans, too. Like plague, it is caused by a rod-shaped bacterium.

Worse, it is now possible to turn *Yersinia pestis* into a deadlier weapon than ever before. Today's scientists can grow the bacterium in quantity in a laboratory. Terrorists would not need fleas to spread laboratory-grown *Yersinia pestis*. An airplane could spray the bacteria, just as crop dusters spray insecticide to kill insect pests. Victims would inhale them, causing the deadliest form of plague.

And the LORD said unto Moses, Say unto Aaron, Stretch out thy rod, and smite the dust of the land, that it may become lice throughout the land of Egypt. And they did so; for Aaron stretched out his hand with his rod, and smote the dust of the earth, and it became lice in man, and in beast; and the dust of the land became lice throughout all the land of Egypt.

—EXODUS, 8:16–19

6 Lousy Lice

We do not like lice. Never have, and never will. Our oldest written records show how we feel about them. In the Bible, lice are the third of the ten plagues God sends to punish the Egyptians for their cruelty to the enslaved Israelites. In many modern languages, the word *louse*—the singular of *lice*—is part of everyday speech. It means something harmful, dirty, and sneaky. A "louse," in English slang, is a nasty person, one you cannot trust. A "lousy" deal is a bad deal. To "louse up" is to make a mess of something.

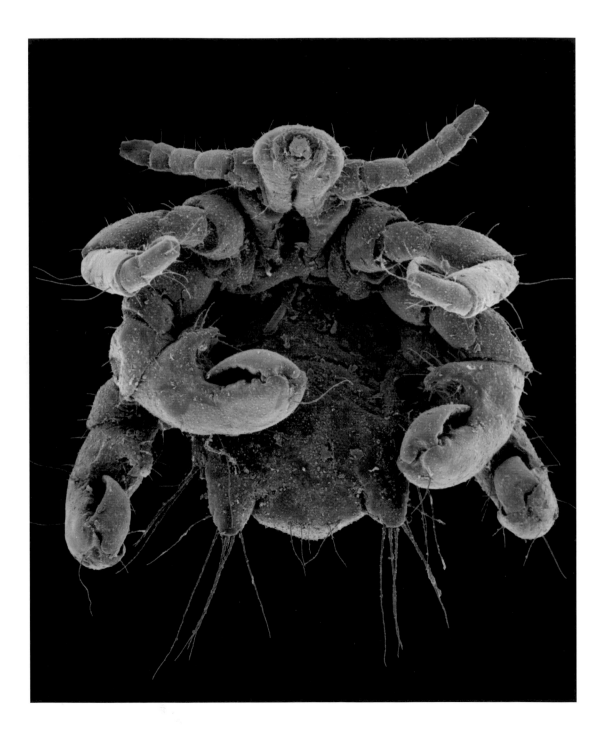

There are over 2,600 species of lice. All are small, flattened, wingless insects varying in color from light brown to dark gray. Unlike fleas and mosquitoes, lice spend their entire lives on a host animal. Lice are slow-moving creatures. While they cannot jump, fly, or run fast, they have stout legs armed with claws for clinging to the host.

The female louse attaches her eggs to a host's hair with saliva that becomes cement hard. Called nits, the colorless eggs are about the size of a knot of fine thread. Monkeys and people get rid of nits and lice by picking them out of each other's hair with their fingers. In English slang, a "nitpicker" is one who harps on tiny details. A "nitwit," in American slang, is very stupid person.

Baby lice do not resemble worms, as the larvae of fleas and mosquitoes do. Called "nymphs," they are miniature copies of their parents and become adults by shedding their skin several times as they grow larger. An adult louse is slightly smaller than the head of a straight pin.

Scientists classify these insects as either chewing or sucking lice. Chewing lice have jaws and feed on bits of dead skin, hair,

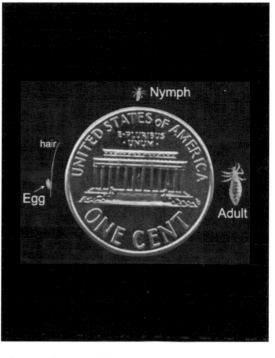

Size of a body louse compared to that of a penny.

Opposite: Body louse

and feather parts. Sucking lice have needlelike mouthparts for piercing flesh and feeding on blood. Normally, both types are fussy, being parasites on just a single host species. Turkey lice favor turkeys. Cat lice favor cats. Honeybee lice favor honeybees, the walrus louse walruses. When a walrus dives underwater, its lice breathe the air bubbles trapped in its fur. Sometimes, however, several louse species share a host, each living in its own special place. Birds may have four species of lice on different parts of their bodies: legs, beaks, wings, and tails. Lice especially like sick or injured animals. For example, a small seabird with a damaged beak had 7,000 lice—at least, that is how many scientists found before giving up the count. A sick fox had no fewer than 14,000 lice on its body!

Lice and people share a long history. Scientists studying 3,000-year-old Egyptian mummies found the remains of lice and nits wedged into the cloth wrappings that encased the corpses. Combs taken from ancient graves in Israel dating to biblical times have the remains of lice in their teeth. "Going over it with a fine-toothed comb" means doing something with great care. The phrase comes from the traditional way of combing out nits and lice.

While we have always disliked lice, some people have found them useful. Centuries ago, Chinese and Europeans treated

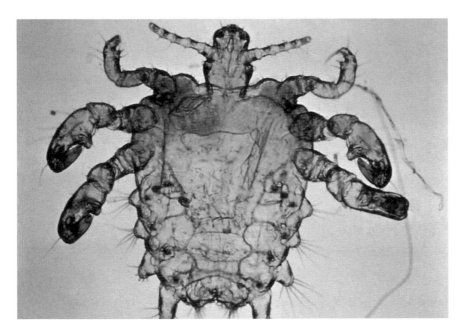

Head louse.

various illnesses with lice. The records do not say if the "treatment" worked. Lice also played a role in government. During the Middle Ages, lice decided town elections in Sweden. Back then, only men with long beards were qualified to run for office in that country; beards, it seems, were signs of wisdom and maturity. In choosing a mayor, candidates sat with their heads bowed and their beards resting on a table. An official then put a louse on the table to "vote." The man into whose beard it crawled got the job! In the 1890s, travelers in northern Siberia, a province of Russia, had an unusual welcome from local tribes. Giggling young women picked lice off their bodies and threw them at the visitors. Sharing lice was their way of proposing marriage.

Head louse egg cemented to a hair.

Human head lice live on the hairs of our heads and necks. Highly contagious, they spread from person to person, especially among groups of children in elementary schools, day-care centers, and camps. Researchers have found that nine- and ten-year-old girls are most likely to get head lice because they go in for group hugs. Sharing hats, combs, and brushes also spreads head lice. Crab lice look like crabs, and live on parts of the body with coarse, thick hair. These include the groin, legs, armpits, beards, eyebrows, and men's chests. Like head lice, "crabs" spread through close contact and shared clothing.

Various medicated shampoos and lotions kill head and crab lice easily. Smearing a child's head with Vaseline, or even mayonnaise or olive oil, suffocates these parasites, though some may survive. While they can cause intense itching, head and crab lice are harmless. Neither carries any disease we know of—yet. Scratching the itch, however, may break the skin, allowing infection-causing bacteria to enter the wound.

That is not true of human-body lice, or "cooties." It seems we did not have these pests until the invention of clothing about 50,000 years ago. Early humans lived in the warm climate of Africa. Since their only "clothing," if any, was plant fibers worn around the waist, they probably did not have cooties. But when humans began moving out of Africa into cooler lands, they had to keep warm. At first, they used fur and leather; later, they learned how to make cloth from wool, cotton, and flax. Somehow they picked up the body louse, and now it lives only on people. Despite the name, it does not live directly on our bodies, but along the seams of our clothes. Adults and nymphs leave their cloth homes to jab

LICE AS MEDICINE

Here are a few louse-medicine recipes from China and Europe:

- To make pounding headaches go away, smear a paste of 300 to 500 ground lice on your forehead
- Relieve toothache by placing a live louse in a hole drilled in a bean sealed in wax and worn around your neck on a string
- To calm an upset stomach, swallow two lice, crushed or alive, with a glass of wine
- Cure malaria by eating three lice with a slice of bread or a plum

Dr. Charles Nicolle

their pointed snouts into our flesh in order to get a meal of blood. These pests can reproduce quickly. Researchers reported that a shirt taken from one person had over 10,000 cooties and an equal number of nits.

Parasitic body lice may also carry a parasite belonging to a group of bacteria called *Rickettsia* (rih-KEHT-see-uh). These rod-shaped bacteria cause a disease called epidemic typhus (TY-fuhs). Next to malaria and plague, epidemic typhus—or simply typhus—is the greatest killer of people in history. *Rickettsia* bacteria release powerful toxins, or poisons, into the human body. These produce a red rash on the chest and back, followed by a blinding headache, fever, and chills. The name *typhus*, from the Greek word for "hazy," well describes the last stages of the disease. High fever (106 degrees F) may last two weeks. During that time, the victim may become dazed and confused, lose consciousness, and die. Unless treated with antibiotics, four in ten victims die; survivors gain lifetime immunity to the infection.

People used to ask the same questions about typhus as they

did about malaria and plague. What causes it? How do we prevent it?

A French doctor unraveled the mysteries of typhus. Like Alexandre Yersin, and Paul-Louis Simond, Dr. Charles Nicolle (1866–1936) had studied under Louis Pasteur in Paris. In 1903, Nicolle became director of a hospital in Tunisia, then a French colony in North Africa. He arrived at his post to find a full-blown typhus epidemic raging. The local hospital was full, nearly every bed holding a typhus patient. Other sufferers stood in lines circling the hospital, waiting for a patient to die so they could take his or her bed.

In Europe, in the 1300s, a woman searches for head lice with a brush.

Dr. Nicolle noticed an odd thing. Those who touched the waiting patients, including medical staff, often got typhus. Yet the moment patients were admitted to the hospital, the infection stopped spreading. While the patients were still sick, no healthy person who visited the typhus wards came down with the infection.

After a while, Nicolle realized that nurses always gave newly admitted patients a hot bath and clean hospital clothing. Yet laundry workers who handled the cast-off clothing fell ill with typhus. It followed that something in the clothes transmitted the disease. So, what did one piece of cast-off clothing have in common with every other piece? Lice!

Nicolle tested his idea by injecting a monkey with blood from a typhus patient. Sure enough, the monkey got the disease. A few days later, he collected a few lice from the infected monkey and put them on a healthy monkey. It, too, developed typhus. Nicolle repeated the experiment several times on different monkeys, but always with the same result. Clearly, lice transmitted typhus.

Further study identified *Rickettsia* as the cause of the infection. Typhus, Nicolle found, passes back and forth between body lice and people. When an uninfected louse sucks an infected person's blood, the bacteria enter its stomach. There they multiply quickly, until the louse's stomach bursts. Before dying, however, the louse may suck the blood of an uninfected person and give them the disease.

Unlike the parasites that cause malaria and plague, *Rickettsia* does not enter a person through a bite. Instead, as the louse sucks blood, it does something truly disgusting. It drops *Rickettsia*-filled feces near the bite wound. The feces dry to a fine, nearly invisible powder. Louse saliva makes the wound itch. Victims then infect themselves by scratching the feces into their skin, rubbing it into their eyes, or transferring it from their fingers to their mouth.

Epidemic typhus is a disease of crowding and dirt. It thrives where people live close together in unsanitary conditions with little chance to bathe regularly or change into clean clothes. This explains its popular names: jail fever, ship fever, and war fever.

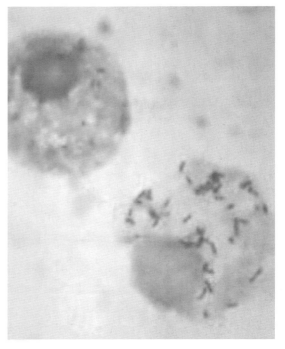

Rickettsia *bacteria that cause typhus.*

It is not easy for a person to be locked up in a jail cell. Not all jails, however, are equal; some are worse than others. Two centuries ago, a jail sentence in Europe and America was often equal to a death sentence. Overcrowded jails were dark, damp, dirty places infested by rats, lice, fleas, and cockroaches. Typhus raced through old-time jails like fire through dry straw.

When infected prisoners stood trial, they brought their lice to court. One famous case took place in 1577. An English prisoner named Rowland Jenks, a printer by trade, faced charges of spreading "false" ideas about religion. Jenks had been in jail for several months, and his clothes were alive with body lice.

The courtroom was packed, onlookers standing shoulder to shoulder for an entire day. Jenks was found guilty, and, as punishment, the judge ordered his ears cut off. Soon afterward, the prisoner took his revenge, although unintentionally. Over 500 of those who had attended the trial, including the judge, sheriff, prosecutor, and jury, fell ill with typhus and died. As if by a miracle, Jenks survived.

Like jails ashore, wooden sailing ships were once crowded and vermin-infested. In early modern times, from about 1400 to 1800 CE, ship captains always tried to sail with twice the necessary crew. This allowed the extras to "fill in" as sailors died of typhus. Often ships returned from a long voyage with a dozen sailors out of the 125 who had originally come aboard. Sometimes the captain and all his officers also fell victim to the disease.

The deadliest typhus outbreaks always came in wartime. In the last six centuries, typhus probably killed more soldiers than all weapons combined. Before an army set out on a campaign, its chaplains prayed that God might spare it from the dread disease. Yet nothing could change the fact that soldiers lived (and live) in close contact with each other, in camps, in trenches, and in foxholes. The longer soldiers stayed in the field, the dirtier they got. Old-time soldiers seldom bathed, as bathing was not the custom; besides, scarce hot water was for tea and coffee, not washing. Lice multiplied, moving from man to man. In quiet moments, soldiers took time out to "read their seams"—hunt for body lice in the seams of their uniforms. Any lice caught exploded with a pop when tossed into a tin can hung over a fire.

When armies surrounded cities, typhus usually broke out in their camps and among those trapped behind the city walls. Sometimes victory did not go to the stronger side or smarter general, but to the side that lost fewer people to typhus. For example, during the invasion of Italy in 1528, a French army laid siege to the city of Naples. Although typhus raged in Naples, the French had to leave when it also struck down 30,000 soldiers in their camps. Thus, typhus killed more French soldiers than enemy swords or cannons.

During the French invasion of Russia in 1812, typhus raced through the army. A soldier wrote in his diary: "I slept for an hour when I felt an unbearable tingling over the whole of my body . . . and to my horror discovered that I was covered with lice! I jumped up, and in less than two minutes was as naked as a newborn babe, having thrown my shirt and trousers into the fire. The crackling they made was like a brisk [shooting]." In the twentieth century, from 1917 to 1921, typhus killed some 3 million people, soldiers and civilians, during the Russian Revolution and civil war. "They died like flies," a newspaper reported.

In 1939, Germany began World War II by invading Poland. Terrified of typhus, the invaders lugged portable showers and laundries to delouse troops and their uniforms. Adolf Hitler, the German dictator, hated Jews and gave orders to kill them whenever possible. Across Poland and Eastern Europe, Hitler's soldiers and police herded Jewish men, women, and children into concentration camps for execution. Conditions were so bad that typhus often took the inmates' lives before the executioners could act. Germans sent Anne Frank, author of the famous *Diary of a Young Girl*, to a death camp where she died of typhus at the age of fifteen.

Strange as it may seem, this awful disease saved lives— once. It happened in 1943, in the Polish town of Rozwadów. As German soldiers prepared to round up the Jews for execution, Eugene Lazowski, the town doctor, staged a fake epidemic. Knowing how much the invaders feared infection, he got samples of dead typhus bacteria from a laboratory. He then injected the harmless samples into healthy people. Told that typhus had broken out in town, the soldiers let nobody in or out. German doctors later demanded blood samples from the "victims." Sure enough, the samples showed that their immune systems had fought off *Rickettsia*, a "sure" sign of infection. Convinced that the town had a typhus epidemic, German forces left it alone for

Spraying a concentration camp survivor with the insecticide DDT to kill lice.

the entire war. Dr. Lazowski's heroic action rescued over 8,000 people from certain death in Hitler's camps.

Though German and Japanese soldiers suffered outbreaks of the disease, no American or British troops got typhus during World War II. This was largely because Allied forces used a newly developed chemical, DDT, to kill body lice. Without waiting for an outbreak, medical teams sprayed the white powder into soldiers' uniforms and civilians' clothing.

Despite these advances, lice are still a problem. In the United States alone, outbreaks of head lice among children account for the loss of 12 million to 24 million school days each year. To fight this menace, many school districts have louse detection programs where health workers inspect pupils' hair and prescribe remedies if the parasite is found. Homeless people in cities are also prone to body lice.

As for typhus, it still haunts the poor mountainous regions of South America, Africa, Asia, and Mexico. The disease is a special menace during the winter months, when people spend more time indoors and do not wash their clothing as often as they should. Yet modern doctors have prevented severe typhus outbreaks with insecticides and antibiotics—so far. Public health officials report fewer than 80 typhus cases a year in the United States. Most cases occur in Texas and California, probably because fleas living on wild squirrels and other rodents in these states can also carry typhus and plague bacteria.

The world has not seen a serious typhus epidemic since the Allies closed Hitler's death camps in 1945. Even so, the danger remains while human-body lice exist.

From the point of view of a tapeworm, man was created by God to serve the appetite of the tapeworm.

—EDWARD ABBEY, American author and activist,
A Voice Crying in the Wilderness, (1991)

7 World's Worst Worms

MEET THE WORMS

One day not very long ago, a researcher sat at her desk at the United States National Parasite Collection in Beltsville, Maryland. She had just returned from Egypt and was eager to study the specimens she had collected there. As she leaned over to look into her microscope, she felt an odd tickling sensation. Moments later, a nine-inch worm slid out of her nose. She must have had it a long time, for worms that size do not develop overnight. Most likely, it was the giant roundworm, *Ascaris*

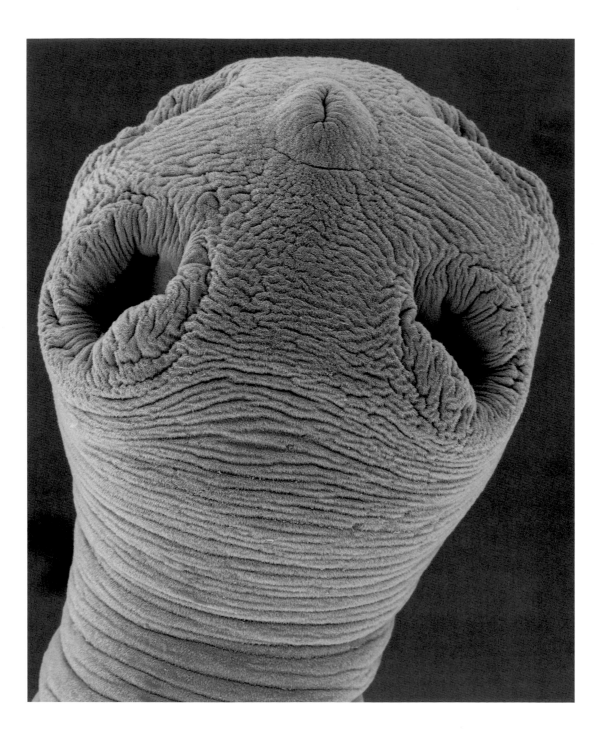

lumbricoides. Yet she was lucky, since this species gets to be 13 inches long, and she had just one. Some people have hundreds of these worms wending their way through their bodies.

Worm is not an exact scientific term. Originally, it meant any long, slender animal without a backbone, arms, and legs. Insect larvae, especially butterfly and moth caterpillars, used to be called worms. So were the fly maggots found in the bodies of dead and decaying animals. In English legend, a brave knight killed a fire-spitting dragon, also called a worm.

Today, scientists apply *worm* to ten large animal groups, or phyla. Most are sea creatures that live in tubes they build on the sandy ocean bottom, or as internal parasites of whales, walruses, fish, and shellfish. On land, most worms live in the soil, like earthworms. Yet some are internal parasites of mammals, including farm animals and humans.

Parasitic worms are called helminths, which comes from *helmins*, the Greek word for "worm." Helminthology is the branch of biology that studies parasitic worms.

So far, we know of 342 helminth species that can live inside human beings. Several different species prefer different parts of our bodies, and all may live inside their chosen spot at the same time without getting in each other's way. Some helminthes favor the muscles, others the bloodstream and

Head of a tapeworm. The indentations on each side are not eyes, but suction cups used to attach it to a victim's intestines. Tapeworms have no eyes.

eyes, and still others the digestive tract. Wherever they live, all parasitic worms belong to two phyla, which scientists classify according to their body shape. Those of the phylum Nematoda (NEHM-uh-tohda) are roundworms. Members of the phylum Platyhelminthes (Plat-ee-HEL-mint-eez) are flatworms. Both groups include monsters, truly the world's worst worms.

ROUNDWORMS

Members of the phylum Nematoda look like bits of spaghetti, except they taper to a point at each end. If you cut one crosswise, you would see that each half is round, therefore the name roundworm. Nematodes have a complete digestive system with separate openings to take in food and get rid of wastes. Scientists have described about 20,000 species of roundworms, such as earthworms, but believe another 500,000 species may exist. In other words, nematodes have the largest number of species in the animal kingdom after insects.

Roundworms live everywhere. We find them on the floors of the deepest oceans and on the slopes of the highest mountains. Some are visible only through a microscope, while others reach a length of three feet. Life on our planet could not exist without them. Like bacteria, they break down decaying plants and animals, returning vital chemicals and minerals to the soil. A handful of soil may contain a million nematodes of various species. One researcher counted 90,000 of them in one rotten apple, and then stopped counting. Nematodes are natural enemies of insect pests like cockroaches and Japanese beetles, and so can be helpful to people in many ways. However, some species of roundworm are harmful parasites of plants and animals, including humans.

Pork Worm

One parasite, the tiny roundworm *Trichinella spiralis*, is common in carnivores, or meat-eating mammals, such as wolves, rats, cats, and bears. The worms' larvae curl up inside cysts, thick-

Trichina life cycle

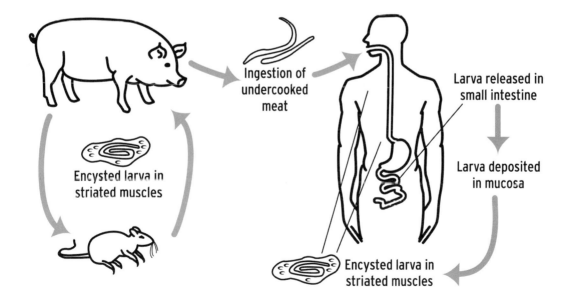

Ingestion of undercooked meat

Larva released in small intestine

Larva deposited in mucosa

Encysted larva in striated muscles

Encysted larva in striated muscles

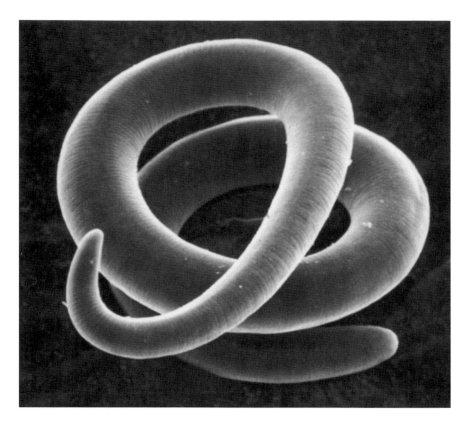

The roundworm Trichinella spiralis.

walled capsules they make to protect themselves from the host's immune system. Cysts look like white beads embedded in the muscles of host animals. When, for example, a cat eats an infected rat, the digestive juices in the cat's stomach dissolve the cyst, freeing the larvae. The larvae then mature and mate. The females lay eggs. When the eggs hatch, the new generation of larvae enters the cat's bloodstream to feed. Finally, they form cysts in its muscles, and then wait for another animal to eat the cat. But time is not on their side. If the cat has a long life, the larvae die, since they cannot break out of the cyst without help from a host's digestive juices.

Trichinella spiralis causes trichinosis in humans, a disease marked by stomach pains, diarrhea, vomiting, and even death. Hunters get the disease by eating infected game. Most people, however, get it from infected pork. Ancient peoples saw a connection between the white "beads" found in pig muscle and trichinosis. Thus, two great religions, Judaism and Islam, have always banned the eating of pork as unclean. In certain conditions, pigs can be very dirty. They may feed on garbage and dead animals; they might also wallow in mud with their own liquefied feces. Yet, we know today that it is easy to avoid trichinosis and still eat pork. Freezing pork for three weeks kills any adult worms it may have. Cooking pork for at least five minutes at over 137 degrees Fahrenheit destroys any cysts in the muscles.

Hookworms

Hookworms are more aggressive than their *Trichinella* cousins. Here, we will let one species, *Necator americanus*, represent them all. The name is Latin for "American murderer." At a quarter inch long, the adult worms look like harmless bits of silk thread. Viewed with an electron microscope, however, they reveal gaping mouths and—teeth! Hookworms are the only worms known to have teeth. Depending on the species, adults have between one and four pairs of triangle-shaped teeth. These parasites latch onto a host's intestines with their teeth, furiously biting into the blood vessels. They have an unlimited appetite for blood.

A female hookworm produces 20,000 eggs a day. After leaving her host's body in its feces, her eggs fall to the ground. If they are lucky enough to hatch in warm, moist, and shaded soil (sunlight dries them out), the larvae wait for a barefoot person to come along. As the person walks by, the young worms gnaw through the sole or the skin between the toes. The person feels nothing, because the larvae's saliva contains a painkilling chemical.

Once inside their host, the young hookworms set out on

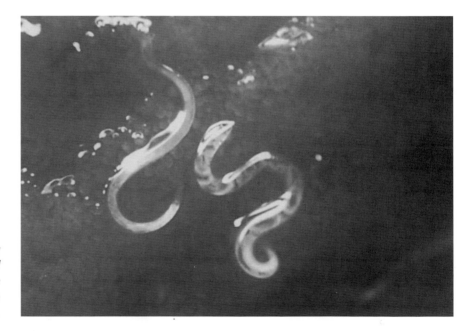

These young hookworms will attach themselves to a host's intestines with their teeth.

a fantastic journey. Biting open a vein, they wriggle inside and dive into the flowing river of blood. Eventually, the vein carries them into the heart where they puncture an artery. The heart then pumps oxygen-rich blood through the arteries throughout the body. Upon reaching the lungs, the young hookworms slice into the air sacks that provide the blood with oxygen, causing severe irritations. These make the host cough up the larvae in mucus, which

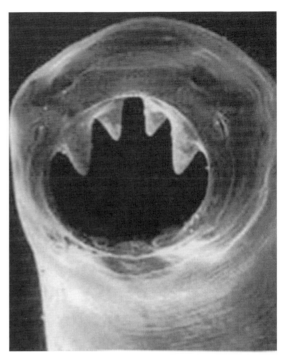

A hookworm shows its teeth.

is then swallowed. Finally, the larvae travel from the stomach to the small intestine, their final destination. They attach to an intestinal wall, mature, and mate. The worms spend 15 years or so in the intestine, feeding and reproducing.

Hookworms infect about a billion people worldwide, mostly in tropical and subtropical countries. That's one-sixth of the human race. Heavily infected people may have thousands of these tiny eating machines in their intestines. Heavy infection causes diarrhea, weight loss, difficulty breathing, and heart problems. Children may also suffer mental retardation because of loss of blood and oxygen to the brain. Doctors use drugs to destroy hookworms and enemas to flush their remains out of the intestines. Needless to say, it is scary to see scores of dead hookworms floating in the toilet bowl.

At least those cured of hookworm can see what ailed them. Victims of the filarial (threadlike) nematode *Onchocerca volvulus* may never see anything again. For they suffer from a disease called river blindness.

River Blindness

According to an African folk saying, "Nearness to large rivers eats the eyes." This is because several species of black fly breed in fast-moving water. While taking blood from an infected person, the buzzing, biting pest sucks up *Onchocerca volvulus* larvae with its meal. The larvae reach maturity in the black fly's body. When it bites an uninfected person, the fly injects the larvae into its victim's bloodstream, where they grow to be adults. Often adult worms attack the eyes, damaging delicate nerves and causing blindness. Some 17.7 million people suffer from river blindness worldwide, over 90 percent of them in Africa.

Elephantiasis

Visitors to tropical lands—Africa, India, and South America— may see victims of yet another disease caused by a roundworm.

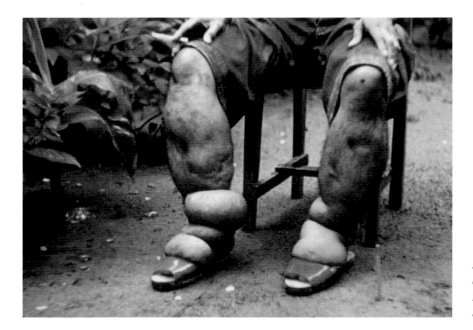

A victim of elephantiasis shows his swollen legs and feet.

Elephantiasis (el-ah-fan-TIE-ah-sis), also called *Wuchereria bancrofti*, infects at least 120 million people worldwide. As with malaria, mosquitoes spread the immature parasites from person to person while sucking blood. Once inside a host, the worms become adults, growing from 1.5 to 4 inches in length.

Adult *Wuchereria bancrofti* curl up in the lymphatic vessels that weave through the body, much like blood vessels. Lymphatic vessels carry lymph, a colorless liquid that contains white blood cells, essential in fighting infections. When the parasites gather in these vessels, they form a living plug. Lymph backs up behind it. Pressure builds. The host's arms and legs swell to twice or three times normal size. Eventually, the swollen areas become

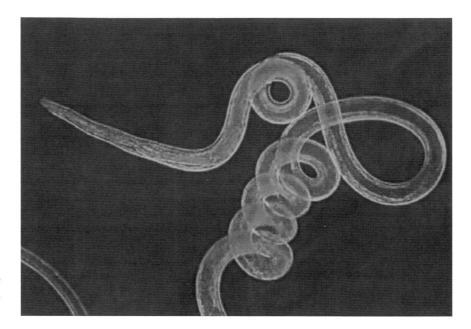

The roundworm that causes elephantiasis in humans.

hard and thick like an elephant's leg, giving the disease its name. Late-stage elephantiasis prevents sufferers from working or moving about on their own. Yet the disease is treatable with medicines, and not usually life threatening.

The Guinea Worm

If we gave worms prizes, the Guinea worm would win the trophy for Nastiest Nematode in Creation. A thing of nightmares, it deserves its Latin name, *Dracunculus medinensis*—"little dragon." This roundworm has tormented humanity throughout recorded history. Its dried remains have been found in Egyptian mummies. It is probably the "fiery serpent" mentioned in the

Bible. This so-called serpent afflicted the Israelites during their wanderings in the Sinai desert after fleeing Egyptian captivity. To this day, African farmers call the parasite "empty granary," because it makes them unable to work at harvesttimes.

Guinea worms are a problem in Africa, Asia, and South America. The trouble begins when a person drinks from a pond swarming with "water fleas," microscopic relatives of crabs and lobsters infected with worm larvae. The person's digestive juices dissolve the water fleas, releasing the young worms into the host's stomach. Quickly, the larvae break through the stomach wall into the connective tissues; that is, the tendons and fat that support the body and hold its organs in place. Soon after

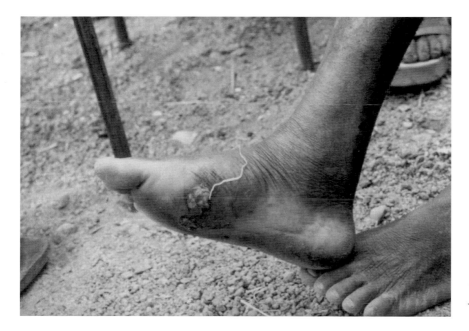

A Guinea peaks out from the burst blister in a man's foot.

mating, the male worms die; the females eat their bodies. A dozen or more females may live in a person, growing thick as a pencil and a yard long.

After a year, eggs hatch inside the female Guinea worms. That is a signal for all sorts of unpleasant things to happen. Their bodies bursting with larvae, the little female dragons move toward the surface of their host's skin. Painlessly, they lodge in the feet, legs, thighs, shoulders, chest, head, and neck. Once in position, however, they release an irritating chemical. A blister forms above each worm, causing unbearable itching and pain. "The pain is like if you stab somebody," said a farmer. "It is like fire [and] you feel it even unto your heart."

By causing such intense pain, the Guinea worm serves its own purpose. For the species to survive, the next generation must somehow return to water. Nature has designed its mothers to help do just that. Within a day or two, the blister opens and a mother worm's head peeps out an inch or so. Her head waves about, feeling the air move over it. Maddened by the itching and burning, victims plunge into pools of water to find relief. As they do, mama worm releases a white liquid from an opening in her head. Yes, she gives birth from her head! The liquid contains thousands of larvae meant for water fleas to eat. To complete their life cycle, the larvae need a person to swallow the water fleas.

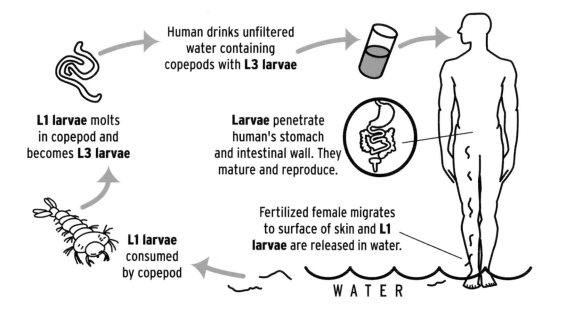

Human drinks unfiltered water containing copepods with **L3 larvae**

L1 larvae molts in copepod and becomes **L3 larvae**

Larvae penetrate human's stomach and intestinal wall. They mature and reproduce.

L1 larvae consumed by copepod

Fertilized female migrates to surface of skin and **L1 larvae** are released in water.

WATER

Guinea worm life cycle

Europeans learned of the Guinea worm when slave traders raided African villages in the early 1700s. There they saw people walking around with sticks attached to white "strings" coming out of various parts of their bodies. This is still the best way to get a little dragon to leave its human host. But it is like holding a bomb with a hair-trigger fuse. Despite the pain, you dare not yank the fragile worm out. For any sudden movement would tear mama worm apart, killing her and leaving the rest of her body to decay inside yours. You would die, horribly, of blood poisoning while rotting from the inside out. Thus, you must keep the stick close by, day and night, waking and sleeping. Dropping it is a death sentence.

In 1986, health workers reported 3.5 million cases of Guinea worm disease worldwide. By 2004, the number fell to a little over 16,000 cases. Thanks to the World Health Organization and private charities, chiefly the Bill & Melinda Gates Foundation, the Guinea worm is well along the road to destruction. These organizations provide special nylon filters to rid ponds and wells of water fleas. The hope is that their efforts will soon rid the world of the scourge of the little dragon. Until then, health workers will continue to remove the female worms the old-fashioned way, by slowly winding them around a stick.

FLATWORMS

Flatworms are members of the phylum Platyhelminthes, a name that comes from the Greek words *platy* ("flat") and *helminth* ("worm"). This phylum contains two major groups: flukes and tapeworms. Together, they number over 15,000 known species. All are parasitic.

Flukes

In Old English, *fluke* meant "flounder," any one of a group of fish that live in salt water. Like the flounder, the worm has a flat oval body. Unlike the fish, this worm also has spines for attaching itself to the inside of a host's body. Most fluke species do not have

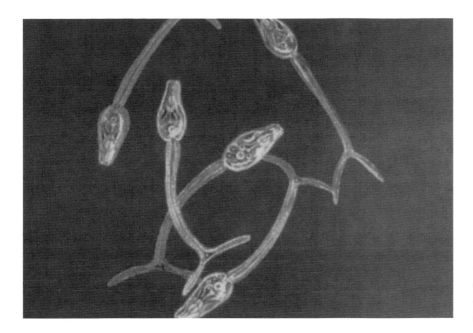

Cercariae (larvae) of an unidentified species of fluke swimming in water.

separate sexes. Individual worms have both male and female organs that allow them, in effect, to mate with themselves. This is a useful arrangement. For a parasite like a fluke, where only one may get inside a host, it might be impossible to find a member of the opposite sex when it is time to mate.

Flukes have complicated life cycles. Most species need two hosts before reaching adulthood in a third or final host. Adults depend on the final host to deposit feces or urine containing their eggs in water. The eggs hatch into larvae that swim by rapidly moving rows of minute hairs along the sides of their bodies. The lucky ones survive by finding a water snail, but most die unlucky. To enter the snail's body, larvae release chemicals that break down the skin on the soft parts outside its shell. After entering the snail, they feed on blood while changing into *cercariae*, the Greek word for "tailed ones." Cercariae are one-eightieth of an inch long with big heads and whiplike tails. Viewed under an electron microscope, they resemble torpedoes.

As cercariae grow, they break out of the snails and follow chemical scent trails left in the water by their second host. Different fluke species favor different second hosts. These may be fish, crabs, frogs, turtles, or even crocodiles. Upon locating their prey, they make a hole in the skin with chemicals and then dive in headfirst. The cercariae must now wait for a third creature to eat the infected host. Only then can they become egg-laying adults.

One group of flukes, the schistosomes (SHISS-tow-soams), differs from the others in a special way. *Schistosome* means "split body" in Greek. Unlike their relatives, schistosomes have separate sexes. The male worm has a groove in his underside, running the length of his body. The smaller female slides her entire body into the groove of her future "husband," somehow locking herself in place. From that moment, they never separate. Bound together as they are for life, not a moment goes by when the couple is not mating. They live this

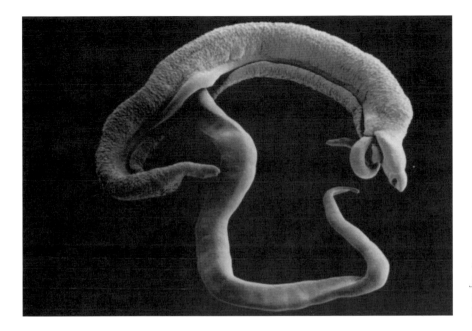

A female schistosome fluke nestles in the special body groove of her lifelong mate.

way unto death, for up to 20 years, producing millions of eggs.

Most schistosomes do not trouble humans unless their cercariae lose their way in the water. For example, after leaving a snail, cercariae of species that need ducks as a second host can accidentally enter the skin of people washing clothes or bathing in lakes. Trapped in the wrong host, the erring cercariae soon die. Still, they cause "swimmer's itch," an annoying rash that goes away by itself in a week. The best way to avoid this condition is by not swimming for long periods in shallow water and quickly drying your skin with a towel after leaving the water. Above all, if you get swimmer's itch, try not to scratch. Try hard, because scratching causes the rash to become infected. Ask a doctor or druggist for an anti-itch lotion or a medicine to make the rash go away sooner.

Blood Flukes

Three schistosome species are serious human parasites: *Schistosoma mansoni*, *S. japonicum*, and *S. haematobium*. Known as blood flukes, each species attaches itself inside the veins that carry blood away from the intestines, liver, and bladder, where urine collects before leaving the body. Humans get blood flukes when the cercariae of these species leave snails and penetrate our skin, thus the popular name *snail fever*. Cercariae can also enter our bodies if a person eats fish or other infected creatures.

Blood Fluke life cycle

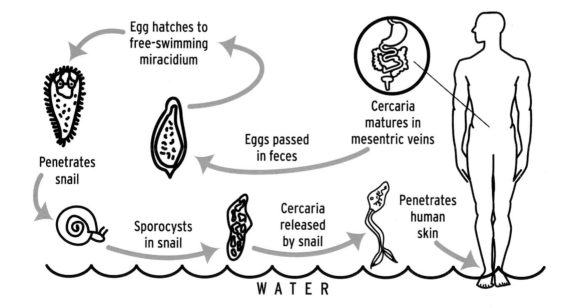

Egg hatches to free-swimming miracidium

Cercaria matures in mesentric veins

Penetrates snail

Eggs passed in feces

Penetrates human skin

Sporocysts in snail

Cercaria released by snail

WATER

Although absent from the Unites States, schistosome disease affects over 200 million people in Africa, the Middle East, Asia, and South America. Its symptoms include high fever, chills, diarrhea, liver damage, and bloody urine. In some parts of Egypt, bloody urine used to be so common in boys that people thought it a natural part of growing up. The parasites damage vital organs; doctors suspect they may even cause cancer of the bladder. As with Guinea worms, the best way to eliminate blood flukes is to destroy the host that carries their cercariae. Governments have created programs to destroy water snails in areas with high rates of blood-fluke disease. Drugs can easily kill any adult flukes in the body.

Tapeworms

Tapeworms differ in key ways from other flatworms. Their name comes from the fact that their flattened bodies resemble strips of packing tape. Larger than flukes, they range in size from the 1.5-inch dwarf to the giant 100-foot whale tapeworm, the longest animal that has ever lived. Just about every species of mammal, fish, and bird can be attacked by at least one species of tapeworm.

Unlike blood flukes, none of the 5,000 known tapeworm species has a mouth or digestive tract. These would serve no

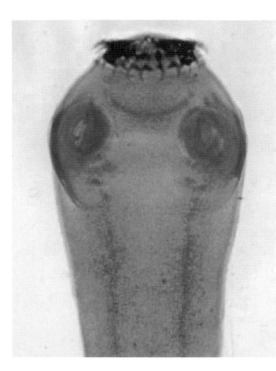

Hooks and suction cups on the head of an unidentified species of tapeworm.

purpose, since the adults spend their entire lives inside a host's intestines, dangling in an ever-flowing "soup" of digested food.

Tapeworms have a simpler body design than flukes. A tapeworm's head, or scolex (SKO-lex), attaches it to a host's intestinal wall. Yet that head is unlike any we are familiar with. It has no eyes, ears, nose, or mouth. It is merely a device for holding on. Depending on the species, the scolex has a variety of hooks, spines, and suction cups. These give the parasite a firm grip despite the wavelike movements of their host's intestines. The worm absorbs nutrients through its skin as the digested food flows past.

A small neck area lies just behind the scolex. This is where all of the tapeworm's body growth takes place. The neck produces egg cases called proglottids (PRO-glot-titz), a chain of rectangle-shaped segments arranged one behind the other. Depending on the species, adults may have several thousand proglottids, each holding up to 40,000 eggs. Since tapeworms, like all flukes except schistosomes, do not have separate sexes, every proglottid contains a complete set of male and female organs for reproduction. As its eggs mature, the proglottid farthest from the neck (the oldest) breaks off and leaves the host's body in the feces. Meanwhile, new egg cases constantly grow behind the neck.

Once outside the host's body, the proglottid dries in the air. Before long, it splits open, releasing its eggs. If an animal swallows an egg while feeding, the egg hatches into a larva that invades a muscle. There the larvae forms a cyst, just as certain roundworms do. If another animal eats the host, its stomach acids dissolve the cyst. Free at last, the larva anchors itself to the intestinal wall, begins feeding, and matures into an adult.

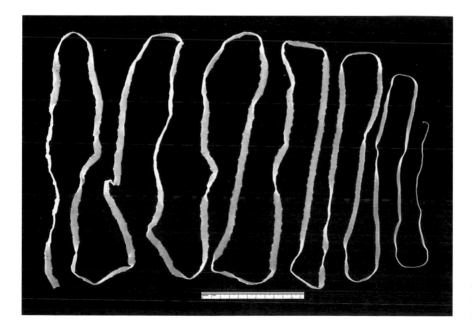

A tapeworm with hundreds of proglottids containing male and female sex organs and eggs.

An adult tapeworm can live 30 years or more.

Five species can infect humans: they are the dwarf, fish, dog, beef, and pork tapeworms. A person gets a fish tapeworm by eating raw or partially cooked fish. This parasite is most common in Japan, where sushi, or raw fish flavored with spices, is a delicacy. Adult fish tapeworms can grow to be 35 feet long, making them the largest human parasites.

Most adult tapeworms, of any species, do not harm humans seriously. This is because they do not attack our bodies, as blood flukes do, but steal only small amounts of food. Often an infected person does not even know they have one dangling inside their intestines. Despite folklore, tapeworms do not

A Brazilian boy, about the year 1930, displays the tapeworms doctors removed from his intestines.

make you hungry, but may cause diarrhea and nausea. About 175 million people worldwide have tapeworm infections.

Only one tapeworm can kill us, and also itself in the process. The adult pig tapeworm, *Taenia solium*, gets to be 10 feet long. If you eat raw or undercooked pork containing cysts, the larvae escape and attach themselves to your intestines in the usual way. The trouble begins if you eat uncooked vegetables with *Taenia solium* eggs on them. Larvae hatch out of the eggs, just as they do in the pig. The bloodstream carries them to every organ of the body, most dangerously to the brain, where they form cysts. Since there are no stomach acids in the brain to dissolve the cysts, the trapped larvae die in their little fortresses. So long as the larvae live, the host's immune system cannot recognize them as invaders. When the larvae die, however, the immune system attacks the cysts, causing swelling. Because the skull is hard, the brain cannot expand to relieve the pressure. The victim develops splitting headaches and dizziness. Increased pressure makes the heart pump harder to deliver blood to the brain, which only further increases brain swelling. Finally, the victim dies of a heart attack or stroke.

You cannot starve a tapeworm. Fasting will make you weak, but not rid you of it. Some experts say it is better to eat foods that tapeworms dislike, like onions and garlic. These weaken the parasite until the scolex loses its grip. Yet it is not pleasant to feel, then see, several feet of squirming tapeworm pass out of the body. Doctors also treat tapeworm infections with drugs. Yet if drugs fail to destroy the scolex and neck, the parasite will regrow itself.

Are Parasitic Worms Good for Anything?

Horrible as they may seem, parasitic worms may do us some good. Recently, researchers suggested that certain illnesses develop when the immune system gets too active, thus damaging the very body it is supposed to protect. Asthma, hay fever, and inflammatory bowel disease are examples of illnesses made worse by an overactive immune system. With inflammatory bowel disease, for example, white blood cells that normally attack an invader target the intestines instead. The result is severe pain, bleeding, and general poor health that may lead to death. This disease afflicts about 600,000 Americans each year.

Around the year 2000, researchers noticed that Africans infected by hookworms were half as likely to get asthma as people in the same area who did not have the parasites. At first, this seemed puzzling. But scientists have long known that parasites may survive in the human body by evading the immune system or damping it down. Perhaps parasites produce a calming effect on diseases caused by overactive immune systems.

Experiments with parasitic worms have shown promising results. Doctors have given volunteer hay-fever sufferers in the United States a drink containing upward of 300 hookworm eggs. "His hay fever," a doctor wrote of one man, "has virtually disappeared." Since hookworms become a problem only if they enter the human body as larvae through the skin, the eggs passed out of volunteers harmlessly in the feces. When people with inflammatory bowel disease drank lemonade laced with 2,500 eggs of the roundworm *Trichuris suis*, their symptoms greatly improved. Here, too, the body safely eliminated the unhatched eggs. In future, some of the world's worst worms may ease human suffering.

8 Avoiding Parasites

We have learned that humans share the world with millions of other life-forms. We share our very own bodies with scores of these creatures, too. Parasites are the most common form of life on earth, and we have discussed just a few of them in this book. Nothing we do will avoid or get rid of them all. That is just the way it is. Most parasites do us little if any harm. Scientists have figured out how to make some help us. But a few are killers.

Bed bug head and upper thorax

Our knowledge of parasites suggests ways of dealing with them. The following methods of avoiding harmful or irritating parasites are mostly common sense and easy to follow. Obeying these simple rules may spare you a lot of trouble and discomfort.

1. PRACTICE GOOD PERSONAL HYGIENE

- Do not touch human or animal feces, for they may contain parasite eggs or larvae.

- Wash your hands well, with soap and hot water, before eating and after using the toilet. There is good reason for the signs in restaurant bathrooms that say employees must wash their hands before returning to work.

- Keep your fingernails short, and clean under them with a brush. This rule is especially important for children, who can self-infect themselves with pinworms. Though these worms are harmless—as far as we know—scratching to relieve the itch can break the skin and introduce harmful bacteria. Females of this common nematode leave the host's intestines to lay eggs around the anus, while spraying a fluid that causes itching. When a child scratches the itchy area, eggs stick to the fingers and get under the fingernails. If the child puts those fingers into the mouth, the eggs find their way into the intestines, where they will hatch. Also, keep your fingers out of your nose. The slightest scratch may break the skin and let harmful bacteria into your bloodstream.

2. THINK BEFORE DRINKING WATER

You need water to live, but you must be careful to make sure the water you drink is safe and clean.

- Never drink from rivers, streams, lakes, or ponds no matter how clean the water may seem. Animals often defecate and urinate in water. Microscopic creatures like water fleas harbor parasites that could wind up inside you. Campers and hikers can buy special tablets to purify "wild" water in sporting-goods stores.

- When swimming, do not swallow any water. Towel-dry as soon as you get out. Afterward, take a shower or bath.

3. BE CAREFUL WHEN PREPARING FOOD

Cooking is more than whipping up tasty, healthful meals. Proper cooking also plays a key role in protecting against parasites.

- Cook meat and fish thoroughly. Similarly, the best way to avoid parasitic worms is by not eating raw or uncooked meat and fish. Nobody wants to play host to an intestinal tapeworm.

- Thoroughly clean knives and cutting boards used to prepare raw meat before putting them away. Bacteria grow on unclean surfaces, which may also harbor parasite eggs and cysts.

- If you like the taste of raw meat or fish, before eating freeze it solid for at least a week or so. Parasites cannot survive deep freezing.

- Eggs and larvae of parasites often cling to plant surfaces. So, if you plan to eat raw fruits and vegetables, wash them thoroughly. Better yet, peel the skin off fruit before eating it.

4. ENJOY THE OUTDOORS SAFELY

When going outdoors, the basic rule is that protecting your skin prevents parasites from burrowing into your body.

- Never go barefoot where animals may have defecated. These places include horse stables, cow pastures, and shady places with warm moist soil such as marshes.

- Do not allow bloodsucking insects, ticks, and mites to get at you.

- Use insect repellent, but check with your doctor or druggist about possible allergic reactions.

- Wear protective clothing in forests, brush, and tall grass. This means a long-sleeved shirt and pants tucked into the elastic tops of your socks. Light-colored clothing is best because ticks are dark, and can be seen more easily when on lightly colored fabric. When coming back indoors, inspect your clothing and shoes for ticks, and shower as soon as possible. Be on the lookout for strange "freckles" that seem to move.

• Should you find ticks on your clothing, pull them off with tweezers. If a tick is biting into you, have a doctor or a responsible adult remove it. Never use nail-polish remover, matches, or other chemicals on a tick. These may force it to let go, but before it does, the tick may vomit into the wound, causing infection.

• Fly maggots have barbed spines on their bodies. Pulling maggots off will tear them apart, but leave the spines embedded in the skin, causing infection. To get maggots to leave, cut off their air supply by smearing the infected area with Vaseline.

5. CHECK YOUR PETS

• Remember that any animal, wild or domestic, can have parasites, and usually does.

- Cats and dogs, our most liked house pets, need flea collars. These help pets stay healthy and prevent their fleas from jumping onto their owners.

- It is not a good idea to let pets sleep on your bed. Sometimes they have worms: hookworms, whipworms, or tapeworms. Worm eggs and larvae may get on sheets and blankets, and from there into you.

- Many pets must be regularly dewormed or given medicines that kill parasitic worms. Ask a veterinarian about what medicine to buy.

- Use separate feeding dishes for your pets. Never let them eat from the same dishes your family uses.

- After a pet licks you, wash the area. It will love you just as much after you wash its saliva off your face.

6. LISTEN TO YOUR BODY

Many parasite infections produce similar symptoms, whatever the specific cause. These include diarrhea, nausea, fever, headache, and fatigue. Yet many other illnesses, such as food poisoning and the common cold, produce the same symptoms. Only a doctor can tell what ails you and how to treat it. If it is suspected that you have a parasite, he or she may take your medical history, test your blood, and examine samples of your feces under a microscope.

Finally, listen to the advice of parasitologist Dr. J. Ralph Lichtenfels: "You shouldn't be afraid of parasites. But you should know about them so you don't do stupid things."

FURTHER READING

History and Science of Parasites

Buckman, Robert. *Human Wildlife: The Life That Lives on Us*. Baltimore: The Johns Hopkins University Press, 2003.

Combes, Claude. *The Art of Being a Parasite*. Translated by Daniel Simberloff. Chicago: University of Chicago Press, 2005.

Drisdelle, Rosemary. *Parasites: Tales of Humanity's Most Unwelcome Guests*. Berkeley and Los Angeles: University of California Press, 2010.

Stewart, Amy. *Wicked Bugs: The Louse That Conquered Napoleon's Army and Other Diabolical Insects*. Chapel Hill: Algonquin Books, 2011.

Zimmer, Carl. *Parasite Rex: Inside the Bizarre World of Nature's Most Dangerous Creatures*. New York: The Free Press, 2000.

For Younger Readers:

Davies, Nicola. *What's Eating You?: Parasites—The Inside Story*. Illustrated by Neal Layton. Cambridge: Candlewick Press, 2007.

History of Parasitic Diseases

Friedlander, Mark P. *Outbreak: Disease Detectives at Work*. Minneapolis: Twenty-First Century Books, 2009.

McNeill, William H. *Plagues and Peoples*. New York: Doubleday, 1976.

For Younger Readers:

Marrin, Albert. *Oh, Rats! The Story of Rats and People*. Illustrated by C. B. Mordan. New York: Dutton Children's Books, 2006.

BIBLIOGRAPHY

Andrews, Michael. *The Life that Lives on Man.* London: Faber & Faber, 1976.

Ash, Lawrence R., and Thomas C. Oriehel. A*tlas of Human Parasitology.* Chicago: American Society for Clinical Pathology Press, 1997.

Berenbaum, May R. *Bugs in the System: Insects and Their Impact on Human Affairs.* New York: Addison-Wesley Publishing Co., 1995.

Buchsbaum, Ralph. *Animals Without Backbones: An Introduction to the Invertebrates.* Chicago: University of Chicago Press, 1948.

Buckman, Dr. Robert. *Human Wildlife: The Life That Lives on Us.* Toronto: Key Porter Books, 2002.

Debré, Patrice. *Louis Pasteur.* Baltimore: Johns Hopkins University Press, 1998.

Desowitz, Robert S. *The Malaria Capers: More Tales of Parasites and People, Research and Reality.* New York: W. W. Norton, 1991.

————. *New Guinea Tapeworms and Jewish Grandmothers: Tales of Parasites and People.* New York: W. W. Norton, 1987.

Dobell, Clifford. *Antony van Leeuwenhoek and His "Little Animals."* New York: Russell & Russell, 1958.

Gross, Ludwik. "How the plague bacillus and its transmission through fleas were discovered: Reminiscences from my years at the Pasteur Institute in Paris," *Proceedings of the National Academy of Sciences*, August 1995, 7609–7611.

Kelly, John. *The Great Mortality: An Intimate History of the Black Death, the Most Devastating Plague of All Time.* New York: HarperCollins, 2005.

Knutson, Roger M. *Fearsome Fauna: A Field Guide to the Creatures That Live in You.* New York: W. H. Freeman and Company, 1999.

————. *Furtive Fauns: A Field Guide to the Creatures Who Live on You.* Berkeley, Calif.: Ten Speed Press, 1996.

Lapage, Geoffrey. *Parasitic Animals*. Cambridge, England: Cambridge University Press, 1951.

Lehane, Brendan. *The Complete Flea.* New York: The Viking Press, 1969.

Marriott, Edward. *Plague: A Story of Science, Rivalry, and the Scourge That Won't Go Away.* New York: Metropolitan Books, 2002.

Martill, David M., and Paul G. Davis. "Did dinosaurs come up to scratch?," *Nature*, December 10, 1998, 528–529.

Riedel, Stefan. "Plague: from natural disease to bio-terrorism," *Proceedings of the Baylor University Medical Center*, April 2000, 116–126.

Rocco, Fiammetta. *Quinine: Malaria and the Quest for the Cure That Changed the World.* New York: Perennial, 2003.

Rosoebury, Theodor. *Life on Man.* New York: Viking Press, 1969.

Spielman, Andrew, and Michael D'Antonio. *Mosquito: The Story of Man's Deadliest Foe.* London: Faber & Faber, 2001.

Di Tura, Agnolo. "The Plague in Siena: An Italian Chronicle," in William M. Bowsky, ed., *The Black Death: A Turning Point in History.* New York: Holt, Rinehart & Winston, 1971, 13–14.

Zimmer, Carl. "Animal Parasites," *Science World*, February 12, 2001.

————. *Parasite Rex: Inside the Bizarre World of Nature's Most Dangerous Creatures.* New York: The Free Press, 2000.

Zinsser, Hans. *Rats, Lice, and History.* Boston: Little, Brown & Co., 1984.

INTERNET RESOURCES

Cox, F.E.G. "History of Human Parasitology," *Clinical Mircrobiology Reviews*, October 2002, 595–612; cmr.asm.org/cgi/content/full/15/4/595

History of the Microscope: campus.udayton.edu/~hume/Microscope/microscope.htm

Robert Hooke: ucmp.berkeley.edu.edu/history/hooke.html

Anthony van Leeuwenhoek: ucmp.berkeley.edu.edu/history/leeuwenhoek.html

Spontaneous Generation: biology.clc.uc.edu/courses/bio114/spontgen.htm